SO-BYH-114

INSIDER'S
VIETNAM
LAOS AND CAMBODIA
GUIDE

DEPARTMENT OF IMMIGRATION
PERMITTED TO ENTER
AUSTRALIA.
24 APR 1986
on
For stay of 12 Month
SYDNEY AIRPORT

IMMIGRATION & ETHNIC AFFAIRS
.........Person
30 OCT 1989
DEPARTED
AUSTRALIA
SYDNEY 32

中华人民共和国
广东省公安厅

上陸許可
ADMITTED
15. FEB. 1986
Status: 4-1- 4
Duration: 90 days
NARITA(N)
Immigration Inspector
日本国

ADMITTED
20 OCT. 1988
Status: 4-1-16
Duration 180 day
Port: HANEDA
Signature

№ 011278

THE UNITED STATES
OF AMERICA
NONIMMIGRANT VISA
ISSUED AT
PASSED
Air Port

HONG KONG
(1038)
−7 JUN 1987
IMMIGRATION
OFFICER

U.S. IMMIGRATION
170 HHW 1710
JUL 20 1983

8 NOV 1992

F.N.X. C.H VIETNAM
THI THUC
N0 306 A 8
NOI BAI

DEPARTURE
17 NOV 1992
VIENTIANE AIR PORT
SIGNATURE

THE INSIDER'S GUIDES

AUSTRALIA • BALI • CALIFORNIA • CHINA • EASTERN CANADA • FLORIDA • HAWAII •
HONG KONG • INDIA • INDONESIA • JAPAN • KENYA • KOREA • MALAYSIA AND SINGAPORE •
MEDITERREAN FRANCE • MEXICO • NEPAL • NEW ENGLAND • NEW ZEALAND • PORTUGAL •
RUSSIA • SPAIN • THAILAND • TURKEY • VIETNAM, LAOS AND CAMBODIA • WESTERN CANADA

The Insider's Guide to Vietnam, Laos and Cambodia

© 1995 Novo Editions, S.A.

Hunter Publishing Inc
300 Raritan Center Parkway
CN94, Edison, N.J. 08818
published by arrangement with Novo Editions SA
53 rue Beaudouin, 27700 Les Andelys, France
Telefax: (33) 32 54 54 50

ISBN: 1-55650-625-2

Created, edited and produced by Novo Editions, S.A.
Editor in Chief: Allan Amsel
Original design concept: Hon Bing-wah/Kinggraphic
Picture editor and designer: Chan Sio Man
Text and artwork composed and information updated
using Ventura Publisher software

Printed by Samhwa Printing Co Ltd, Seoul, Korea

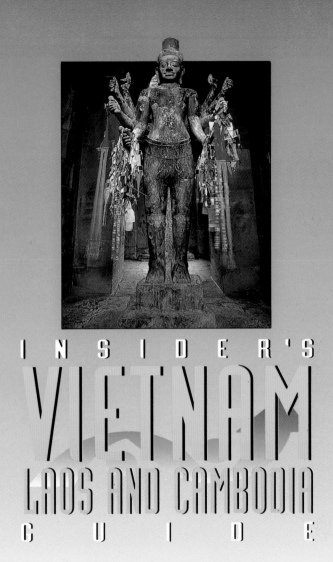

INSIDER'S
VIETNAM
LAOS AND CAMBODIA
GUIDE

By Derek Maitland

Photographed by Alain Evrard

HUNTER PUBLISHING, INC.
Edison, N.J.

Contents

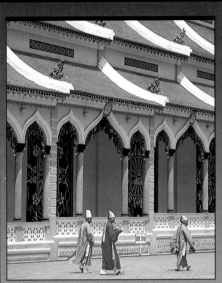

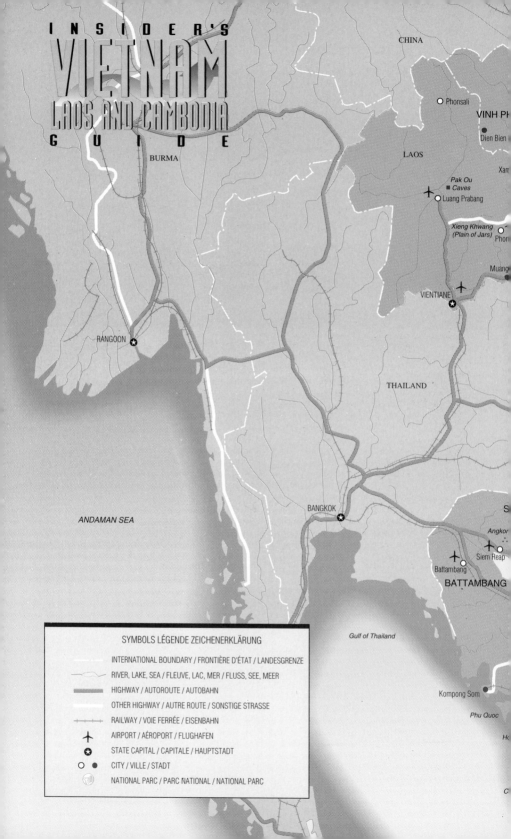

Welcome
to
Indo-China

ON ONE of my most recent visits to Vietnam, I was traveling from Hanoi to Haiphong when a flash of light — something as swift and elusive as a fish rising and diving in a lake — caught my eye in the rice paddies that flank the road just beyond the capital's urban limits. I stopped the car and took a closer look, and watched a rural ritual that's become something of a dream for Asia travelers in this era of burgeoning industrial economies.

On a grassy dike alongside an irrigation stream stood two gnarled old women, each everyday rituals of rural life — traditional farming techniques that have given way to mechanization in many other areas of Asia — that are almost a kind of ballet, a folk art. I watched for different irrigation techniques, in particular, and found that they varied from region to region. In other areas of the north, the bamboo basket became a heavier wooden scoop hung from a bamboo frame and rocked back and forth with the same endless rhythm, like a baby's cradle, to hurl the water from one paddy to the next. On the road between Danang and

accompanied by a younger woman who was obviously their daughter, or daughter-in-law. Working as two teams, they faced each other on the dike, bending and swaying in a sinuous, almost hypnotic rhythm — each couple pulling on woven bamboo ropes attached to a wide-mouthed bamboo basket. As they swayed forward, the basket sank into the irrigation canal. As they pulled back it lifted, full of water, and with an almost imperceptible flick of the wrists they made it flip and dash its contents into an adjacent rice field. It was the water, splashing in the morning sunlight, that had caught my attention on the road.

This was something I was to see time and time again throughout Vietnam, the

Hue in the northern central region of what used to be South Vietnam, I came across two old people — husband and wife — sitting side-by-side on a bamboo contraption in their wide-brimmed conical bamboo hats and pedaling a wooden machine with a paddle-wheel that scooped the water into a small field of rice seedlings. From a distance they looked like lovers sitting together in the golden, late afternoon sun. When I approached them and talked with them, they had the same friendly, guileless charm that I was to find in the countryside right across Indo-China — a charm that's all the

LEFT: Tending the rice fields, Vietnam's Meking Delta. ABOVE. Beach vendor, Qui Nhon, Vietnam.

more striking and enjoyable when you consider not just the brutal, backbreaking reality of peasant life but the long shadow of conflict and suffering that lies behind the color and exoticism of this entire region. And it's this juxtaposition of charm, antiquity and epic struggle that makes this area the most culturally fascinating new destination in Asia. Indo-China, one of the most beautiful and most cultured regions of Asia, has a turbulent and often violent history which extends more than 2,000 years into its past.

If we consider just these two millennia alone, the three countries that make up this beleaguered region — Vietnam, Laos and Cambodia — have been engaged in almost continuous internecine wars and major struggles to survive in the shadow of their powerful neighbors, China, Siam (Thailand) and Burma.

Centuries of conflict have given them a tenacity which has been most dramatically evident in their heroic, if devastating, contemporary struggles — against the French, who colonized Indo-China from the late 1800s, and against the Americans, who decided in the early 1960s that the toppling dominoes of communist expansion would be halted in the jungles, mountains and fecund rice-plains of this tragic region. The brilliant victories scored against both these Western powers have only heightened the sense of tragedy. Military triumph has won Indo-China the political and cultural independence that its three territories have been seeking for centuries, but at a tremendous cost: in each case, victory has placed them under hard-line revolutionary socialist rule, resulting in nearly two decades of social purges, isolation, austerity and virtual economic collapse.

Now, as these three countries re-open their economies to the rest of the world, the tragedy is even more pronounced. Unique cultures which for many years have been overshadowed by war — remembered as monochrome glimpses of fear, agony and flight in the violent melee of gunships, rockets and bombs — are suddenly striding with all their color and exoticism onto the world stage. But they are backward, sometimes derelict societies, robbed of their sophistica-

tion and competitiveness by the post-war revolutionary crackdown, now racing to catch up with a region-at-large which has become the world's new economic powerhouse.

But it's this agony and ill-fated heroism of Indo-China that gives it such a powerful mystique, and such tremendous potential as Asia's new travel and tourism frontier. A great pilgrimage is already under way — perhaps greater than the initial rush to visit "forbidden" China when it first re-opened its doors from 1979. What's attracting it is the savage romance of Indo-China's twentieth century struggle — those monochrome images of parachutes bursting like cotton buds over the smoke and carnage of the French collapse at Dien Bien Phu; the bellies

of the American B-52s splitting open to shower their excrement down, down, down into the jungled hills and rice-paddies of Vietnam and Laos; the naked girl virtually roasted alive by napalm; the police chief blowing the Viet Cong prisoner's brains out for the press photographers in Saigon; the panic and chaos of the American withdrawal from South Vietnam in 1975; the sheer horror and atrocity of "Year Zero" that began with the Khmer Rouge victory in Cambodia.

Can such terror and suffering possibly be called romantic? Certainly not in the popular sense of the word. Even the most hardened and cynical war veteran, Indo-China "hand" or Vietnam fetishist, drawn back with the first waves of visitors to the

scene of such darkness and iniquity, is undeniably reconciled to the deathly stupidity of the two Indo-China wars. Yet for many of them, it is just as painfully undeniable that these were momentous experiences, however deep the scars it left on their lives—and Indo-China's 17 years of post-war isolation and stagnation have made it all the more difficult to cast them aside.

The French colonial architecture is still there, crumbling and leaking and often turned into ramshackle public housing, or faithfully preserved here and there as a government office or cultural monument. But it's certainly there — the beautiful

ABOVE: Sampan vendors on the Perfume River in Hue, Vietnam's ancient capital.

old Municipal Theater, more commonly known as the Opera House, in Hanoi; the elegant central Post Office in Saigon, with its main hall reminiscent of a cavernous Victorian railway station; a fading but particularly stately mansion which is now the home of the Lao Revolutionary Museum in Vientiane; the Auberge du Champa, another antique French mansion now resurrecting itself as a thoroughly memorable hotel in Pakse in southern Laos; the weather worn but picturesque terraces and old public buildings of the

former royal capital of Laos, Luang Prabang, nestled among the golden spires of Buddhist wats as though a sleepy French provincial town had been lifted up and set down in Shangri-La.

These are examples of the French heritage that spring immediately to mind, just touching briefly upon the wealth of old homes, halls, ministries, commercial buildings, churches and cathedrals, and bridges that still exists throughout Indo-China. In some respects, they are a testament to the culture of the revolutionaries who fought so ferociously to throw off the colonial yoke that they represented — finally swarming in their thousands over the last, battle-worn French defenders of Dien Bien Phu in May, 1954. Traveling through Indo-China today, it's almost as if the relics of colonialism have been just as fiercely preserved — though it's probably more realistic to consider that

within the alternating cycle of war and austerity that's gripped the region right up to this day, there's been little time or money to pull the old French infrastructure down and build a new one in its place.

Time has certainly lent romance to this era of Indo-China's agony, and among the foreigners now flooding into the region, particularly Vietnam and Laos, there are many old French paratroopers, Legionnaires and colonial officials who, like everyone else, finally have the chance to return to the battlefield. For the veterans of what Vietnam now calls the "American War," time hasn't yet healed all of the scars. For them, the pilgrimage is not so much romance as a conflicting concoction of pain and pride — pain for what went on in the years 1962–75, an inescapable pride at having survived it. What's left of the Vietnam War has nothing of the French charm — rusted, stripped helicopter gunships, some left where they crashed in the countryside, others mounted outside the war museums; a crudely sculpted stone plaque alongside Truc Bach Lake in Hanoi commemorating the shooting down of a United States aircraft in 1974; the former United States Embassy in Saigon, still clad in its anti-rocket facade, left empty, falling into ruin, as though to remind the world how high-tech military power failed against an agrarian bamboo culture. From the air, you can still make out the craters left by countless B-52 bombing raids over the Plain of Jars in Laos. Flying into key airports throughout the region, you can see rolling clusters of concrete shelters and revetments which once housed American F-4 Phantoms and other warplanes. At the top of a hill called Phu Si in Luang Prabang, right next to Wat Chom Si, you'll come across an old Russian anti-aircraft gun that was presumably installed after the communist Pathet Lao victory. Then there are the war cripples and amputees, thousands of them, especially in Vietnam and Cambodia. Then there's Cambodia itself, a living testament to that terrible conflict, still armed, still divided between communist Khmer Rouge and moderate forces and still threatening, even now, to erupt into what may possibly be the final battle of Indo-China.

ABOVE: Bridge over the Perfume River, Hue.
OPPOSITE TOP: Hilltribe village on the Ha Giang River, Vietnam. BOTTOM: Sunrise at Dien Bang near Da Nang.

For many veterans in this new tourist pilgrimage, Indo-China is an emotional experience, a coming to terms, a healing of wounds; and it's reflected in the desire to make amends that's drawn some of them back — groups of vets building a clinic outside Danang, a school near Phonsawan, the new tin-roofed "capital" of Xiangkhwong province in Laos, home of the Plain of Jars. The old capital, Xiangkhwong, was virtually destroyed by bombing in the war. But for all visitors, whether they were part of the war or not, there is something about

Indo-China which cannot be found anywhere else in the world — the juxtaposition of horror and beauty, the region that was engulfed on the one hand in one of the most savage, destructive wars in history and is now, in peacetime, unveiling a mystique, exoticism and charm that were virtually lost in the clamor of TV news reports and newspaper headlines in the past.

Right across the cultural spectrum, Indo-China is re-introducing the world to its rich history and culture — magnificent Hindu and Buddhist temples and relics like fabled Angkor Wat in Cambodia, the Cham ruins

ABOVE: Cham ruins at Phan Thiet, Vietnam.
RIHGT: Idyllic rural scene, Phan Rang, Vietnam.

in Vietnam and the region's oldest Buddhist landmark, Wat Phu in Laos; evocative traditional dance and, particularly in Vietnam, unique musical instruments that have been virtually unseen through the war years; dramatic natural attractions like the offshore karst formations of Vietnam's Halong Bay and the Plain of Jars in Laos, which have been off-limits for decades; some of the most beautiful countryside in Asia, in Vietnam's Central Highlands and vast Mekong Delta region, and in the rugged mountains and plateaus of Laos; colorful rural life in which traditional farming techniques, particularly the ubiquitous water buffalo, take you back to an image of Asia that's fast disappearing elsewhere; and the people themselves — friendly, still relatively cosmopolitan and glad to see foreigners again, generally imbued with a sense of relief that the worst is now over and that things can only get better from now on, and universally anxious to put the past behind them and catch up economically with the rest of the world.

In this sense, Indo-China still stands in something of a time-warp, its architecture and infrastructure frozen by the isolation that the region slipped into after the war, and by the trading and financial embargo imposed by the Americans after the communist victory in Vietnam. For returning veterans and Indo-China devotees, this has meant something quite remarkable — probably the first generation in history that's able to go back to a scene of such significance and find, after so many years, in an era of such rapid global development, that nothing essential has changed. For newcomers, Indo-China offers the same opportunity — to explore vibrant, little-known cultures in which time has virtually stood still since the guns of war were officially silenced 20 years ago.

For old war correspondents like me, this return to the battlefield, this second chance, has been one of the most wonderful events of my life. To see and study the exoticism, industriousness and charm that were simply shadows beyond the smoke and fear of the war — that has enriched my own life and confirmed a deep love and fascination for this tragic, beautiful region which I'm sure you, the new Indo-China traveler, will feel too.

Welcome to Indo-China

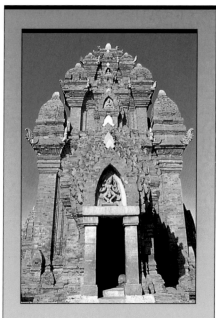

The Cultural Collision

ARCHAEOLOGISTS have found evidence of human settlement in Indo-China, mainly in what is now north Vietnam, as early as 500,000 years ago. But it wasn't until the thirteenth century BC, during the Bronze Age, that anything approaching sophisticated tribal life appeared — and again, it was in the coastal plains of Vietnam, beyond the hardships and terrors of vast jungle-clad mountain chains that march up from the northern fringe of the Mekong Delta into landlocked Laos.

THE ANCIENT HINDU KINGDOMS: FUNAN AND CHENLA

By the time of the birth of Christ, the first of two great cultural pressures was beginning to give shape to Indo-China. Hindu influence, which was to sweep the region from India to Indonesia, established the kingdom of Funan in what is now southern Vietnam and eastern Cambodia. And all at once, the region leapt for the first time into international prominence.

From the first to sixth centuries, absorbed into the vast trading empire that India had created, Funan literally put the Indo-China peninsula on the map — enjoying prestigious and far-flung trading contacts with India, China, Indonesia, Persia and even the Mediterranean. In one of those discoveries that makes any historian's heart leap, archaeologists have unearthed a gold Roman medallion in Vietnam's Kien Giang province, where Funan's capital was located, dated 152 AD and inscribed with the bust of Emperor Antoninus Pius, the successor of Hadrian. This early internationalism, and the colonial era that came much later, has a significant bearing on Vietnam's economic renaissance today: the south, particularly, has a long tradition of trade and cultural exchange with the rest of the world.

While Funan was in its heyday, another Indianized domain, the Hindu kingdom of Champa, arose to the north in the coastal area of what is now Danang. While Funan has left an important commercial legacy, Champa's legacy to Vietnam remains its most illustrious cultural relics — the Cham ruins, the remains of 15 temple towers, at

My Son near Danang, and a collection of stone images and sculptures in the city's Cham Museum.

By the eighth century, Champa dominated much of what is today central Vietnam and had extended its rule as far south as Phan Rang. But it was constantly at war with the southward-migrating Viets to the north, and these in turn were engaged in a long-running struggle for survival against imperial China.

THE CHINESE IMPACT

The Vietnamese themselves, though, originate in Eastern China in an area now covered by the provinces of Jiangsu, Zhejiang and

Fukien. Until the king of the state of Chin unified China in the third century BC, China was a collection of independent kingdoms, two of which were called Yueh and Min-Yueh. "Yueh" is the Chinese word for "Viet," the ideogram comprising the radical for "roam" with the word "bandit." The two kingdoms were known for their irreverence and failure to observe the norms of traditional propriety — Confucius grumbled in the fifth century BC about their lascivious women and vulgar music. "Yueh-nan" or "Vietnam" means the Southern Viet, and south they went, spurred on by the efforts of the king of Chin (who was now the Emperor of China) to secure their obedience. They migrated into Champa, Funan and Chenla, conquering and absorbing the local population as they went. Many Cambodians and Laos would argue that the trend has not stopped. In spite of their resistance to Chinese domination, Vietnam's culture still owes more to Chinese traditions than those of either Cambodia or Laos.

The Chinese had conquered the Red River Delta in north Vietnam in the second century BC, triggering a fierce resistance among the Vietnamese that still underscores relations between the two countries today. While relations between Hanoi and Beijing are now normalized, with both clinging to the collapsing pedestal of socialism, they fought a short but bitter border war as

ABOVE: Statues of mandarins guard the Khai Dinh imperial tomb in Hue, Vietnam.

recently as 1979 and have yet to settle their rival territorial claims to offshore oil deposits in the South China Sea.

The first most memorable battle against Chinese central rule was fought in the year 40 AD by the Trung Sisters, two high-born Viets who led a rebellion that re-established sovereignty over the Red River Delta. Three years later the Chinese counter-attacked, grabbed the region back, and the two vanquished queens committed suicide; but they've gone down in history as Vietnam's most revered heroines, and even today you'll find key streets named Hai Ba Trung in Hanoi, Saigon and other major cities.

For more than 800 years, right up to the tenth century, the Chinese maintained and strengthened their grip on today's northern Vietnam, naming it Annam ("pacified south"). There were various Vietnamese rebellions during this period, but it took the collapse of the T'ang dynasty and China's preoccupation with chaos and power-struggles within other parts of its realm, to give the Vietnamese the advantage in the field. In 938 the Chinese were finally routed in a revolt led by Ngo Quyen. A thousand years of Chinese imperial rule came to an end, and Ngo established the first of 12 dynasties that were to maintain Vietnamese sovereignty and independence, despite various internal conflicts, until it fell under French domination in the mid-1800s.

But it must be remembered that for much of this time, what we now regard as Vietnamese sovereignty applied only to the northern region. The state of Champa continued to dominate what was to become central Vietnam and part of the south right up until the eighteenth century, creating a cultural division between north and south that has been most vividly emphasized in modern times by the 1954 partition of the country and the Vietnam War, and is even quite evident today. As for Funan, we'll see that it simply disappeared into the maw of the Khmer empire, based in Cambodia, which controlled the Mekong Delta until this vast, rich rice bowl was brought under Vietnamese suzerainty in the seventeenth century.

Well preserved Cham tower dating from the sixth century at Po Nagar, near Nha Trang, south Vietnam.

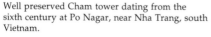

Nor did the landmark battle of 938 see the last of northern invaders. In the thirteenth century the Mongol Yuan Dynasty, the heirs of Kublai Khan's savage conquest, invaded northern Vietnam twice in a bid to get their hands on Champa. They were soundly defeated on both counts, and two more great warriors joined the ranks of Vietnam's resistance heroes — Tran Hung Dao, whose statue stands today, high on a pedestal in Saigon's "Hero Square" facing the Saigon Floating Hotel, and Emperor Ly Thai Tho, better known as Lei Loi, whose

more benign Mekong River Valley and either settling there or continuing on into what is now northeast Thailand. Five hundred years later another migration began, this one fleeing Mongol troops sent into China's Guangxi and Yunnan provinces to bring troublesome non-Han populations to heel.

While the Thais settled right through northern Laos and Thailand, they clung together in separate tribal groups, each with its own leader. But in the mid-thirteenth century the clans in northern Thailand organized themselves in rebellion against the

name has joined that of the Trung Sisters on several main streets throughout Vietnam.

THE ARRIVAL OF THE MOUNTAIN PEOPLE

While Chinese pressure to keep its empire intact can be said to have welded Vietnamese nationhood, it was the crucible from which neighboring Laos sprang. It's known that there was a human presence in this largely mountainous wilderness some 10,000 years ago. But around the eighth century the first of two major migrations by Thai-Kadai tribes from southern China began trickling through the steep hills, finally reaching the

Khmers, and in doing so established the kingdom of Sukhothai. In a series of pacts with Thai warlords in Chiang Mai and Phayao, Sukhothai rule was able to extend right across the Mekong to include Wieng Chan (City of the Moon) whose name the French later romanized into Vientiane.

Thwarted in northern Thailand, the Khmers now gave their backing to the man who could well be called the father of Lao nationhood — Chao Fa Ngum, a warlord from Muang Sawa (later known as Luang Prabang). Fa Ngum seized Wieng Chan from the Thais and then marched on into Thailand itself; and in 1353 he established the kingdom of Lan Xang (Ten Thousand Elephants) embracing the Khorat Plateau of northeast Thailand and much of what is the state of Laos today. But Fa Ngum didn't stop there — he pushed Lan Xang's borders eastward to the Annamite Mountains of Vietnam and even threatened the kingdom of Champa, which unnerved his ministers so much that they deposed him and booted him into exile.

Fa Ngum's successors consolidated what was now a powerful kingdom and the embryo of Lao nationhood. But when one king, Setthathirat, went missing in 1571 after a military foray into Cambodia — thought to have been slain by unpacified hill tribes in

pincer, with the Thais of Siam on one side and the Vietnamese on the other — each of them intent on claiming this strategic mountain domain as a vassal state.

THE BIRTH OF THE KHMER EMPIRE

At this stage of Indo-China's history, with Vietnam comprising two relatively powerful independent states and Laos torn apart by internal rivalry, it's time to look at the third key element of the saga, Cambodia. From the first

southern Laos — Lan Xang fell into 60 years of chaos in which the Burmese, from the north, took the opportunity to pick bits of the kingdom off for themselves. Finally, a new iron leader, King Suliya Vongsa, arose out of the turmoil in 1637 and, in the ensuing six decades — the longest reign of any Lao monarch — pulled the warring Lao factions back together, re-established firm centralized rule and made Lan Xang more powerful than it had ever been before. This was the kingdom's golden era, its Elizabethan age. The trouble is, King Vonsa died in 1694 with no son to succeed him, and this first virtual Kingdom of Laos literally fell apart into three warring territories. More than that, the Laos found themselves caught in a deadly

The Cultural Collision

to sixth centuries, much of what is now Cambodia was part of the Hindu kingdom of Funan, and it shared the region's brisk trade and cultural intercourse with the outside world. But in the middle of the sixth century, the reign of the Khmers began — an age of explosive expansion characterized by conquest and tremendous cultural development.

In the middle of the sixth century a tribal force called the Kambujas from the middle Mekong region established a new kingdom called Chenla. This state then turned its attention east, to the rich Mekong Delta area, and began to absorb Funan. Two centuries

OPPOSITE: Van Kiew tribal village in the Cam Lo Valley. Central Vietnam. ABOVE: Young fisherwoman in Danang.

27

later, Chenla broke up into rival northern and southern kingdoms. Civil wars broke out in the south as rival leaders fought for power, weakening the region so much that it attracted invasion and annexation by Hindu forces from Java.

It took two attempts to sever Cambodia from Javanese rule, which was all-powerful in the region at the time. The first try by a Khmer prince ended in short order when the king of Zabag (Java) mounted an expedition to Cambodia and beheaded him. The second effort was made in 802 by Prince Jayavarman II, who declared himself independent of Java from his mountain fastness at Phnom Kulen, the first capital of Cambodia. The Javanese were unable to bring the Cambodians to heel and in ignominy watched the rapid growth of a great imperial power under Jayavarman. More importantly, he established a dynasty in which successive kings built upon the firm centralized administration that he'd set up. The result was the Khmer empire—which by the twelfth century had brought a large part of Vietnam, Laos and Thailand under its control and had even subjugated the kingdom of Champa.

This move against Champa was rash and ill-fated: Cham armies struck back in 1177, destroyed Angkor and very nearly wiped out the Khmer empire with it. And had a Khmer strongman not stepped into the breach at this point, Cambodia would not possess one of the great cultural wonders of the world today.

The empire's savior was King Jayavarman VII, who ascended to the throne in 1181 and immediately began restoring Khmer stability, sovereignty and power. But his fame rests in the new symbol of Khmer power that he built — Angkor Thom. Many people today think of Angkor as Angkor Wat, built by Suryavarman II (1112–1152) — a single, particularly spectacular temple ruin, albeit one of the most important on earth. But what Jayavarman VII built was a huge new capital, Angkor Thom, with a population of more than one million, an intricate network of canals, dams and irrigation systems and Angkor's most celebrated monuments, the awesome Bayon Temple, the Baphuon and the Terrace of Elephants.

An important point worth noting is that in spite of the greatness of the Cambodian

Empire, it was fatally flawed with a mysterious problem that shaped its policies and sowed the seeds of the monstrous brutality which reached its apogee under the Khmer Rouge. Its people seemed incapable of producing sufficient progeny to maintain the population or provide adequate labor for the great engineering works being undertaken at the time. The consequence was that the only way in which the Khmer kingdom could maintain its population level and get enough laborers was to launch an endless succession of wars on its neighbors, not in order to acquire territory but to obtain slaves who were atrociously treated. Far from being a new phenomenon, the Khmer Rouge are the inheritors of the darkest side of an ancient and glorious history (The only

contemporary account of life in Cambodia in those days survives as notes made by an "ambassador" of the Mongol court in Khanbaliq — later called Peking — who was in fact a spy named Chou Ta-kuan. He was sent to assess the possibility of Mongol conquest, and his advice was "You haven't a hope!" But his notes make hair-raising reading.)

Reinvigorated by all this grandeur, the Khmers embarked on another period of conquest and avenged their humiliation by the Chams by driving deep into Champa and ultimately destroying this proud central Vietnamese state. But then, as with the Lan Xang empire of Laos, Khmer power waned with the death of its iron man. With the loss of Jayavarman VII, Angkor gradually fell into decline and the Khmer state found itself weakened in

the face of an onslaught by the rising new power of Southeast Asia — the Thais.

By the end of the sixteenth century, both Cambodia and Laos were virtually fighting for their lives, threatened and squeezed by the Thais and the Vietnamese. Both states remain trapped to some extent in the same vice today, with Vietnam and Thailand competing for cultural, political and economic dominance of them. In Laos, the death of King Suliya Vongsa in 1694 and the collapse of the Lan Xang state eventually led to Vietnamese control of Wieng Chan (Vientiane) and the Middle Mekong region and Thai control of Champasak to the south, a rich

Angkor Wat temple ruins — the sacred city had a population of over one million in its heyday.

agricultural plain close to modern-day Pakse. It was when the Thais began confronting the Vietnamese in Wieng Chan, exacting tribute alongside their rivals, that Lao subservience ended. The area's warlord, Prince Anou, boldly declared war on the Thais, with disastrous results: the Siamese destroyed Wieng Chan, then marched on Luang Prabang and Champasak, and by the closing years of the eighteenth century had occupied and virtually depopulated most of the country, forcibly resettling the Laos in northeast Thailand.

In Cambodia, Siamese attacks began in the thirteenth century after the death of Jayavarman VII, but it took the Thais more than 200 years to secure the prize they were after — the vast treasure house and seat of Khmer power, Angkor. It was in the mid-fifteenth century that they finally overran the temple city, forcing the Khmers to move their capital to the vicinity of what is now Phnom Penh. The Khmers fought back, and at one stage managed to push their forces to the Siamese capital of Ayutthaya; but in 1594 the Thais conquered Phnom Penh, and the great age of Khmer power and prestige was finally brought to an end.

What is equally significant about the Khmer collapse is how it introduced a completely new political and military element into the Indo-China arena, and one which would have a profound effect on the region in the future. Pressed by the Thais, and with Phnom Penh about to fall, the Cambodians became the first Indo-Chinese to call upon the Western powers for help. The request went out to the Portuguese and Spanish, the first Europeans to explore Asia, but when a Spanish expedition from Manila finally came to the rescue it was too late — Phnom Penh had already been conquered by the Thais.

Instead of turning on the Thais, or returning to Manila, the Spanish decided to stick around. They then became so deeply embroiled in Thai-Cambodian intrigues that the Khmers eventually had to do a complete turnabout and enlist Thai help to get rid of them. In 1599 the entire Spanish garrison in Phnom Penh was massacred, and a Thai puppet monarch put in power. From that point on the once-powerful Khmer state was ruled by a succession of beleaguered monarchs who were under such intense pressure from rivals that they had to seek Thai or Vietnamese help to stay in power.

But these were costly alliances: the Vietnamese began their takeover of the southern Mekong Delta region — once a Khmer domain — in return for their assistance, and the Thais grabbed control of Battambang and Siem Reap provinces. Not only that, they grabbed the Khmer royal family, too, actually crowning one Khmer monarch in their own capital Bangkok and then installing him in power at Udong, a temple city close to Phnom Penh. Indeed, the Khmer state — and modern Cambodia — might not have prevailed at all, had it not been for the timely, if infamous, intervention of yet another foreign power which has had the most abiding contemporary influence on Indo-China — the French.

THE FRENCH

The French colonial experience in Indo-China followed the rather bumbling tradition of European colonialism across the globe — exploration, followed by trade, followed by missionaries, then culminating in military action to protect the merchants and evangelists from the inevitable cultural backlash. And this is almost exactly how the French stumbled into Vietnam.

Although Portuguese, Dutch and French traders and missionaries had been active in Vietnam since the sixteenth century, the French were the first to become involved militarily there. We've read how a series of 12 dynasties, beginning in 938, were able to maintain sovereignty and a measure of stability in northern Vietnam, with the kingdom of Champa flourishing in much the same state in the central-south. In 1765

Hue, proclaiming himself emperor and raising an army to kick the Chinese out — which he did in 1789, routing them in a battle near Hanoi which earned him a revered place in Vietnam's military hall of fame and established yet another tradition of heroic street-names.

But while Nguyen Hue was saving the north, a prince named Nguyen Anh, usurped by the Tay Son rebellion, was plotting revenge in the south. After getting nowhere with the Thais, Nguyen Anh made elaborate overtures to the French for mili-

the Tay Son rebellion, led by three brothers from a wealthy trading family and aimed at corruption and maladministration, put an end to the status quo. Within eight years, the Tay Son rebels had overrun southern Vietnam, killing 10,000 Chinese residents of Cholon in what is now Saigon in the process, then they went on and conquered the north.

At this point, the route to French dominance of Vietnam gets a bit complicated, but I can assure you that it all becomes clear in the end. First of all, the emperor installed in the north by the Tay Son rebels turned out to be a weakling who called in 200,000 Chinese troops to help him maintain power. This led to one of the rebel brothers, Nguyen

tary assistance, even sending his four-year-old son to the court of Louis XVI as a gesture of good faith. The support that he got was tacit, but enough to give him the edge over the Tay Son. With the help of two warships and 400 French mercenaries, Nguyen Anh crushed the Tay Son, captured Hanoi, proclaimed himself Emperor Gia Long and set about rebuilding the war-ravaged country. More significantly, he united Vietnam — north and south — for the first time.

Emperor Gia Long consolidated and developed Vietnamese nationhood during

OPPOSITE: Ceramic bas-relief at Wat Phnom, Phnom Penh records the ceding of the province of Battambang to Cambodia in the Franco–Siamese treaty of 1907. ABOVE: French colonial architecture. Hanoi.

his reign from 1802 to 1819, but he and his two successors, Minh Mang (1820–1841) and Thieau Tri (1841–1847) were hardly visionary or progressive leaders. Supported by traditionalists, they ruled Vietnam with a whip in one hand and the rigid precepts of Chinese Confucianism in the other. They didn't like foreign missionaries, whom they regarded as a threat to the Confucian state, and when they began executing Vietnamese Catholics and expelling Jesuit scholars and priests they triggered a gathering clamor in France for intervention to stop the repres-

sion. It was when several foreign missionaries were put to death in 1858 that the French — who had helped put the Nguyen dynasty in power, after all — finally stepped in, attacking Danang with a force of 14 ships and then moving south to capture Saigon.

As with most colonial expeditions, once the French toe was in the bath there was no stepping back. Spurred by Vietnamese resistance on the one hand and efforts to open the society to trade and evangelism on the other, the French waded deeper and deeper into the region, first subduing the south then seizing the Red River Delta and Hanoi and finally imposing a Treaty of Protectorate on the imperial court in Hue. By 1887, the colonial takeover of Vietnam was complete — and, as subsequent events have shown, the seeds of the first Indo-China war were already sown.

It was not just Vietnam that had come under French rule; by this time Laos and

ABOVE: Old colonial administrative building, Saigon. OPPOSITE: Saigon's most enduring landmark, Notre Dame Cathedral.

Cambodia were also part of what the French proclaimed as the Indo-Chinese Union. In Laos, the French had been welcomed as an ally against the Thais, and their legation in Luang Prabang became the launching point of a campaign to push the Siamese right out of the country. By 1907, the Thais had pulled back across the Mekong River and Laos was a full French protectorate.

Cambodia's absorption into the union was inevitable, linked economically with Vietnam's Mekong Delta and providing a buffer, with Laos, against the kingdom of Siam. In 1863 the French persuaded the Cambodian monarch, King Norodom, to sign a treaty of protectorate, and 11 years later another agreement was coerced which gave the French full colonial power.

As harsh and unpalatable as it may now seem in this post-colonial age, French rule brought some benefits to Indo-China. Colonial administration, though paying lip service to a series of puppet monarchs in each country, brought modernized government to the region and an infrastructure of roads, railways, communications and institutions which is still quite clearly evident today. The French also put a stop to expansionism in the region, and this gave Cambodia and Laos their first real sense of security for centuries. While French military power kept the Thais at bay to the west, Vietnam's imperialist ambitions were also thwarted.

THE SEEDS OF REVOLT

It's probably because of this protection that both Laos and Cambodia gave the French very little trouble during what could be called the idyllic years of colonial rule. Resistance was minimal, and occasional rebellions were directed mainly at corrupt or harsh native officials rather than the French. But both countries paid the price of foreign occupation — their cultures and traditional institutions submerged by the weight of French administration, education, religion and undeniable sense of superiority. While newly-emerging middle classes welcomed French ways, an underlying vein of anger and resistance obviously existed — ultimately exploding with brutal fury in the

Khmer Rouge pogrom, directed at virtually everything foreign, sophisticated or even educated, in Cambodia.

Vietnam was a much different kettle of fish. From the very beginning of French rule there was fierce and often widespread resistance — not surprising when set against the tremendous battles that had been fought through the centuries to keep China at bay. As in the other Indo-China states, there were Vietnamese who came to terms with and even flourished in the transplanted French culture — particularly the ruling elite, bu-

From the turn of the century right up until World War II, the French found themselves in almost continual struggle against nationalist movements. The Japanese victory over Russia in 1905, and the 1911 to 1912 republican revolution in China, heartened the dissidents. The rise of an urban proletariat and a growing corps of students who'd been free to study in France and other Western nations eventually produced the one political force with the manifesto, dedication and organization capable of leading the nationalist

reaucrats, merchants and sections of the armed forces and police — but much of the vastly agrarian population found itself laboring under the yoke of a system set up to economically exploit the country and its people. In times of rebellion, and there were many intrigues and uprisings, French reprisal was often brutal. The guillotine was imported to deal with extremists — providing one point on which the Vietnamese have never forgiven the French. One of these awful contraptions is on show today in the grounds of the War Museum in Saigon.

cause — the communists under Ho Chi Minh.

After organizing strikes, unrest and uprisings against the French for more than two decades — and coming under increasingly fierce French reaction — the Vietnamese communists found the opportunity they'd been waiting for when the Japanese occupied Vietnam and Indo-China in World War II. Working with the Viet Minh — the name of these nationalist guerrillas taken from the League for the Independence of Vietnam (Viet Nam Doc Lap Dong Minh Hoi) — they were the only force to seriously resist Japanese rule. In 1944, the Viet Minh were receiving finance and military aid from the Americans, and thereby hangs a

ABOVE: Young soldiers at Liberation Day parade, Danang.

The Cultural Collision

tragic tale: Ho Chi Minh thought he would get United States blessing for full independence after the war, and the Americans neglected an opportunity which would have saved both nations from the savagery of the Vietnam War in later years. In September 1945, with the Japanese defeated, the Viet Minh controlled so much of Vietnam that Ho Chi Minh was able to declare independence and proclaim the establishment of the Democratic Republic of Vietnam. What happened then was an act of almost obscene political cynicism on the part of the victorious Western powers.

The Chinese were given the task of disarming the Japanese north of the 17th parallel in Vietnam, and the British were assigned to the south. The Chinese went on a rampage in the north, and Ho Chi Minh had to accept French help, of all things, to halt their pillaging. In the south, the British not only used defeated Japanese forces to help maintain public order — it was soon clear that their main task was to help French regain colonial power. The Americans stood by and did nothing.

INDEPENDENCE AND THE FIRST INDO-CHINA WAR

Within weeks, the French were ruling Vietnam again, but by now the lust for independence was too strong. In early 1947, some weeks after a vicious French attack on opposition elements in Haiphong, serious fighting broke out in Hanoi and the first Indo-China war began.

It took the Viet Minh eight years to drive the French out of Vietnam for good, and the character and strategy of the combat was virtually a preview of the second, far more destructive, war to come. The French received massive American military aid. The Viet Minh fought a war of attrition, a guerrilla campaign, which combined shrewd military and political action — their political agenda based on growing disenchantment and opposition to the war in France itself. When victory finally came at Dien Bien Phu in May 1954 — the Viet Minh pouring in their thousands from trenches and emplacements after laying siege to the French posi-

tions for nearly two months — it was an ignominious end to the French empire in Indo-China: the 10,000 or more soldiers and Legionnaires who surrendered were not just demoralized but starving, virtually abandoned by their compatriots back home.

It seems astonishing today that the French fought so fiercely to retain Vietnam when they'd already divested themselves of the rest of Indo-China by the time they made their last stand at Dien Bien Phu. Laos had been granted full independence in 1953 against the background of complex political maneuvering that threw up two nationalist figures who were to have a significant impact on the country's future course — Prince Souvanna Phouma, a neutralist leader, and the leftist Prince Souvanna Vong, who sought support from the Vietnamese communists for a revolution under the banner of the Lao Patriotic Front, or Pathet Lao.

In Cambodia, another now-familiar figure had strode onto the national stage — Prince Norodom Sihanouk, proclaimed king by the Vichy French during the Japanese occupation and still enthroned when the country gained full independence along with Laos in 1953. Sihanouk later abdicated, allowing his father to become king, but virtually ruled Cambodia as prime minister and head of the all-powerful People's Socialist Community party until the monarch died in 1960. Then he made himself chief-of-state. Although a self- proclaimed neutralist, Sihanouk's conceited, self-centered policies — in which he treated Cambodia and its people as his personal property — created the seedbed, as we shall see, for left-wing revolution in Cambodia — and the dark agony it ultimately suffered under the Khmer Rouge.

The full independence of Vietnam, Laos and Cambodia was officially ratified by the Geneva Accords of July 1954. But while these agreements left Laos and Cambodia intact, they divided Vietnam at the 17th parallel, with the despotic Ho Chi Minh's communists ruling the north and an equally despotic, United States-backed anti-communist, Ngo Dinh Diem, controlling the south. One of Diem's first official acts was to renege on the Geneva Accords, refusing to take part in nationwide elections which had been dictated in the agreements. He held a referendum instead, asking voters whether he should continue to rule the south. Amid claims of rabid vote-rigging, he won a resounding "yes" and proclaimed himself president of the Republic of Vietnam. The United States and most of its traditional European and Asian allies immediately recognized his regime, underscoring the 17th parallel as the line that had been drawn against further communist expansion in the region.

16,000 United States military advisers, sent in by the Kennedy administration, were already trying to prop up a southern political infrastructure that was to remain every bit as repressive and corrupt as the Diem regime.

A year later, Kennedy was dead, two United States warships had come under what they claimed was an "unprovoked" attack in the Gulf of Tonkin off North Vietnam and President Lyndon Johnson had launched a massive bombing reprisal against the North. And the Vietnam

THE SECOND INCO-CHINA WAR AND THE AMERICANS

With Diem's rise to power, the die was cast for American involvement in Vietnam and inevitable war. Diem soon proved so corrupt, repressive and politically paranoid that he became an embarrassment to Washington and was overthrown and murdered in a United States-backed coup in 1963. But by now, Hanoi had launched its military campaign to liberate the south and reunite the country; Washington's bid to halt the toppling dominoes of communist expansion had become a crusade, with Vietnam its chief battleground; and more than

War — the second Indo-China War — had begun.

The Vietnam War lasted 11 years, and the terrible cost to both sides — the Americans and the Vietnamese — has been evident since the last shot was fired and will be debated for decades to come. Its savagery deeply undermined the American public's faith in its own ideals and institutions and spawned a high-level political philosophy, espoused by a succession of presidents — Johnson, Nixon and, later, Ronald Reagan — that anything goes if it means containing communism. Defeat cost America its belief in its own righteousness and invincibility, much of its global prestige and its supremacy in Asia, not to mention 58,000 servicemen killed in action and almost double that number who have committed suicide for various war-related reasons at home since.

For Vietnam, victory — as heroic as it was — cost an estimated four million civilian lives, along with hundreds of thousands of military casualties in the North and South. And while it re-established national sovereignty and pride, it put the communists in power, with the political and social repression and "cleansing" inevitable under hard-line, embittered revolutionary rule. More than that, it closed Indo-China's doors to the rest of the world for some 15 years, during which a series of copybook Marxist social and economic experiments virtually bankrupted the three economies. In Vietnam's case, the American trading and financial embargo, imposed after the fall of the South in 1975, denied it access to desperately needed World Bank, IMF (International Monetary Fund) and ADB (Asian Development Bank) loans for reconstruction and development. If there is an epitaph to be written on the Vietnam War, it is the war that nobody really won.

We can look back today with terrible fascination at the litany of tragic events, misconceptions and mistakes that made the second Indo-China War such a global trauma. The American bombing campaign against North Vietnam, which began in 1963 and continued throughout the war, pitted high-technology against a well-organized agricultural society, with relatively little industrial capacity, which was able to repair roads, bridges, dams and dikes as fast as they were damaged. When the first United States Marines were deployed in Danang in March 1965 — spearheading President Johnson's massive build-up of American forces in South Vietnam — the stage was already set for the ultimate failure of mechanized, main-force warfare against an elusive, highly mobile guerrilla enemy.

The United States and ARVN (Army of the Republic of Vietnam) rural pacification program, aimed at isolating the communist Viet Cong guerrillas and destroying their infrastructure, simply led to the wholesale uprooting of thousands of rural families from their ancestral homes and left them to lan-

guish in armed resettlement camps. The strategy of search-and-destroy, an attempt to hunt down and eliminate Viet Cong and infiltrating North Vietnamese units, generally floundered in confusion — for who was to say with certainty who were Viet Cong and who were government loyalists in a population that all looked the same? Moreover, a CIA-operated covert war called the Phoenix Program which employed intimidation, terror, torture and assassination in a bid to fight the communists on their own terms — and which virtually governed the

pacification program throughout the conflict — got so badly corrupted and out of hand that it victimized and alienated millions of neutral Vietnamese.

The Americans lost the political war, too. Much of the failure of the Phoenix Program — as infamous as it was — has been attributed to the discreditable caliber of leadership that Washington supported, namely presidents Nguyen Cao Ky and Nguyen Van Thieu who are alleged to have used the pacification scheme more against their rivals than the communists. If we take the key political blunder that the American

OPPOSITE: Vietnam flashback — panic at the United States Embassy in Saigon as communist troops close in. ABOVE: Government tanks in Da Nang.

military hierarchy made, it was assuring an already uneasy American public back home that the war was practically won, that the "light at the end of the tunnel" could be seen, as early in the conflict as 1967. The communist Tet Offensive of January 1968, however costly it proved in communist lives, blew open the credibility gap between the Pentagon and the public, cut the heart out of American support for the war and turned the United States anti-war movement into a national cause. From that point on, the American involvement in Vietnam was more a prolonged tactical retreat.

Perhaps the most disastrous step taken by the Americans was President Richard Nixon's invasion of eastern Cambodia in April 1970, an offensive aimed at destroying Viet Cong border sanctuaries and easing pressure on the United States in the Paris peace negotiations. Up until that time, Cambodia and Laos had been sidelines to the main conflict in Vietnam — though Laos had sustained an American bombing campaign estimated among the heaviest in history.

At the start of the American build-up in Vietnam in 1963, Laos had been in turmoil, with three political factions, including the leftist Pathet Lao under Prince Souvanna Vong and Prince Souvanna Phouma's neutralists, jockeying for power. In 1964, after a series of failed attempts to form coalition governments, Souvanna Vong pulled out of what he regarded as a rigged match and took his guerrilla forces into the mountains. American military advisers moved in to support the government, a massive bombing operation was unleashed against Pathet Lao bases and infiltration routes and the CIA raised an army of specially trained Hmong hilltribe warriors and Thais for covert operations.

THE KHMER ROUGE HORROR

In Cambodia, United States involvement came about partly as a result of Prince Sihanouk's struggle to stay in power. In the early days of the war he declared Cambodia neutral, but then turned around and severed diplomatic relations with Washington but

allowed North Vietnam and the Viet Cong to use Cambodian border areas as a sanctuary and infiltration zone. In 1967, he did another about-turn: facing a rural rebellion against his autocratic rule and convinced that the communists were out to get him, he began cracking down harshly on leftists. Two years later, the United States launched devastating B-52 bombing raids against guerrilla base camps in eastern Cambodia. In March 1970, Sihanouk was mysteriously deposed while on a trip to France by a rival faction led by General Lon Nol. Now he changed his political colors once again, taking up exile in communist Beijing at the head of a rebel Cambodian movement which he had dubbed the "Khmer Rouge."

Richard Nixon's invasion of Cambodia in April 1970 triggered savage warfare between the Khmer Rouge and Lon Nol's government forces. It raged for five years, and despite American military and economic assistance, the Lon Nol regime was no match for the rebels, commanded by a French-educated revolutionary whose name has since become synonymous with genocide, Pol Pot. When Phnom Penh fell to the Khmer Rouge on April 17, 1975 — two weeks before the communist victory in Vietnam — these fanatical Maoist revolutionaries, characterized by their black peasant uniforms and traditional red checkered scarves, wreaked a barbarous revenge on their people.

One only has to visit Cambodia today to see the damage and horror that the Red Khmers inflicted during their demented four-year purge of Cambodian society. Proclaiming "Year Zero" as the start of a complete restructuring of Cambodian society, the revolutionaries virtually closed down Phnom Penh, forcibly evacuating most of its people to the countryside to work as slave labor on farming and rural development projects. Families were broken up, the parents separated and forced into work units that were often many kilometers from each other, the younger children placed in political education camps.

Meanwhile, thousands upon thousands of people were consigned to what has now become a morbid catchphrase of Cambo-

dia's darkest hour — the "killing fields."
Almost the entire intelligentsia and middle
class were wiped out, the victims, some of
them mere children, imprisoned, interro-
gated and brutally tortured before being
taken to rural mass execution spots where
they were put to death — their skulls
smashed with hammers and pickaxes to
conserve ammunition. There is no need for
me to relate more about this wholesale
murder, except to add that between one and
three million people are believed to have
perished at the hands of the Pol Pot regime.
It takes just one visit today to the Genocide Museum in Phnom Penh — formerly
one of the key interrogation centers — and
the genocide monument erected over one
of the killing fields 15 km (nine miles) from
the city, to sense the terrible chilling darkness that swept across the country at that
time.

VIETNAM INVADES CAMBODIA

In December 1978, after a series of Khmer
Rouge border provocations, Vietnam invaded Cambodia, mercifully putting an
end to the pogrom. While it's highly unlikely that humanitarian aims triggered
the invasion — the Khmer Rouge had
been liquidating thousands of ethnic Vietnamese living in Cambodia — the outcome was another quite shameful show
of international cynicism. China and the
United States, both alarmed at the prospect of Vietnamese expansion in Indo-
China, supported the Cambodian rebel
factions, including the Khmer Rouge. Thailand, equally nervous about Vietnamese
power, became the sanctuary for Red
Khmers and other rebel groups forced
westward by the occupation.

The Vietnamese behaved relatively well
during the 11 years they controlled Cambodia, providing a period of security in which
the country could recover from the trauma
of the Khmer Rouge "revolution." In 1989,
under tremendous pressure to mend its
political fences with the rest of the world —
particularly the United States — and reopen
its society to foreign aid and investment,
Vietnam withdrew its forces from Cambo-

dia. The United States immediately severed
its support for the Khmer Rouge and instituted its so-called "road map" of moves —
orchestrated in concert with the hunt for
American MIAs, or servicemen still missing in Vietnam — to establish diplomatic
relations with Hanoi.

THE AFTERMATH

In September 1990, the United Nations
Security Council instituted what was hailed
as a major step toward eventual peace and
stability in this war-weary nation — setting
up a Supreme National Council in which a
coalition of Vietnam-backed government
figures and the major rebel groups, including the Khmer Rouge, would run the country while preparations were made for national democratic elections. The interminable
Prince Sihanouk returned in triumph from
Beijing to head the council, and immediately
starting plastering huge portraits of himself
all over Phnom Penh. Some 15,000 United
Nations troops and rear echelon from nearly
30 countries were deployed in Cambodia to
help rebuild the country's infrastructure,
disarm the rebel factions, resettle thousands
of refugees from Thailand and supervise the
May 1993 elections.

The elections in mid-1993 saw Sihanouk
seeing to his own interests as usual: he was
appointed King and his son prime minister.
The elections were predictably boycotted by
the Khmer Rouge, consensus not being relevant in their mode of government. Allowed
to pour back into Cambodia, they have dug
in again, controlling virtually all the northern half of the country. Backed by Thai
political and business interests deeply involved in lucrative logging and gem mining
in their territory, they launched increasingly
daring attacks on United Nations positions.
More than that, they continue the program
that they launched in 1975, executing and
assassinating whole communities of ethnic
Vietnamese in their area.

If they butcher their way back into power
and are able to manipulate Cambodia's political agenda, this evil force could plunge
Indo-China into yet another era of violence
and agony.

Indo-China Today

THE PEOPLE

If you were to take an emotional common denominator of the three societies of Indo-China, it is that they are all tired of war, deprivation and heavy-handed discipline and are fiercely determined to build a better life for themselves.

Their exhaustion manifests itself in a most surprising and admirable way: in Vietnam, for example, it's difficult today to persuade most people to talk about the war. For all its horror and suffering, they've put it behind them. Their focus is on the future. And to me, this illuminates the inherent strength of their culture—their ability to turn their back on a trauma that still, after all these years, provokes pain and a measure of hostility in the United States.

What's equally surprising is the attitude that today's Vietnamese, Laos and Cambodians have toward foreigners. They're genuinely friendly and hospitable, pleased to see you back in their midst and anxious to learn everything they can about you and your life back home. In many respects, this is the result of nearly two decades of isolation — they've all got so much catching up to do. The social restructuring that took place after the communist victory has a lot to do with it, too. The surviving intelligentsia in each society seems to be reaching out again, trying to recover the worldliness and sophistication that it lost in the post-war disruption. The students are hungry for information and the foreign lifestyles that they're now able to witness on TV. Night schools right across the region are packed each evening with young people studying what they see as the three key subjects of modernization — English, computer studies and business management. The rural people are enjoying, for the first time in many years, a contact with foreigners who aren't leaping out of helicopters and carrying guns.

They're meeting foreigners from everywhere these days — Japanese, Taiwanese, Koreans, Hong Kong Chinese, Singaporeans, Australians, British, Europeans — but they have a particularly ironic passion for the Americans. They're generally pleased to see the Americans coming back, and for a mixture of cultural, economic and emotional reasons. More than one Vietnamese war veteran, for instance, has expressed to me what I think is the underlying mood of the region as it rejoins the world community — that they won the war but lost the peace, simply putting the communists in power.

Years of hard-line revolutionary rule and economic mismanagement have taken their toll throughout Indo-China, producing a region that's regarded as one of Asia's poorest yet has probably the highest literacy rate — something like 88 percent in Vietnam alone — of the so-called Third World. And it is this sense of indignity which is driving the fundamental changes that are taking place throughout Indo-China today, as it strives to close the yawning gap that separates it from other much richer, rapidly developing Asian economies.

If you count the Vietnam War and its outcome as the cultural emancipation of Indo-China, then the second great liberalization began in 1986 when Vietnam's Communist Party, alarmed at the stagnation that the country had floundered into, launched perestroika-style economic reforms aimed at attracting foreign investment and boosting trade. All at once, the doors to Indo-China began to reopen; but, more significantly, rigid internal controls were relaxed — most notably, the government's ban on private enterprise.

It is this freedom to operate a business, to trade and farm for profit, which has most rapidly transformed Vietnam's society and those of its Indo-Chinese neighbors in recent years. It's turned Hanoi from a strictly disciplined citadel of Marxism — a city which, as one foreign joint-venture manager recalls, "rolled up the sidewalks and went to bed at eight o'clock each night" — into a bustling marketplace. Nowadays, Hanoi is literally humming day and night with business, the Old Quarter around Silk Street and the cavernous Dong Xuan Market packed with shops and street-stalls selling everything from Chanel and Lancôme cosmetics to Japanese rice-cookers and electric fans. One of the city's key thoroughfares, Hai Ba Trung,

OPPOSITE: Candlelit procession around Vientiane's most sacred stupa climaxes the That Luang rites.

joint-venture enterprises. They've also tightened the political reins somewhat on the south, unnerved at the prospect of Saigon, particularly, getting out of control.

But despite the government's paranoia, surveillance and occasional crackdowns, the Vietnamese are enjoying what could justifiably be called a new flowering of their

is similarly crowded with stores selling TV sets, VCRs and stereos.

Free enterprise has unleashed such a tremendous torrent of business and trade in Saigon that the pace and character of the city is changing virtually day to day — returning swiftly to the frenzied, free-wheeling center of capitalism that it was during the Vietnam War. Even more spectacular is the vast beehive of business that the city's Chinatown, Cholon, has once again become, fattened with investment money poured in by Chinese family connections in Hong Kong, Singapore and Taiwan.

Saigon has picked up so rapidly from where it left off in 1975, its largely unrepentant capitalists moving so smoothly back into business, that it's been attracting up to 80 percent of the foreign investment committed to Vietnam. While it's obvious that this would happen — the city retaining the expertise needed to drive the country's economic reconstruction — it's also worried the policy-makers in Hanoi. Their response has been to offer special incentives to divert investment to the poorer north, including tax exemptions for the first five years for

culture and society. They're still desperately poor by modern Asian standards — their per capita income currently around US$200 a year, compared with US$8,000 in Taiwan and US$27,000 in Japan — but at least they're beginning to restore cherished traditions and, more importantly, have a bit of fun.

Social restrictions have loosened up along with the economy, reflected by the number of dance halls, discos, karaoke clubs and bars which have sprung up in Hanoi, Saigon and Vietnam's other major cities. In Saigon the bars are called "cafes" or "cafeterias," but most of them are no less hedonistic than their wartime predecessors, staffed by a new generation of bar-girls and hostesses pouring out of the rice paddies to pat, fondle, chat up and hopefully bankrupt new troops of foreigners. Saigon's derelict racetrack is flourishing again, the ponies thundering around it every Saturday ridden by young preadolescent jockeys

ABOVE and OPPOSITE: Four faces of Vietnam — "beginning to enjoy life again".

who look hardly big enough to climb up into the saddle.

People are eating out again — you can see them of a Sunday afternoon dining in open-air restaurants that have reopened alongside Hanoi's sprawling West Lake. New restaurants are opening up everywhere, especially in Saigon, where you can take your pick of good Vietnamese, French, Italian, Chinese, Japanese or Korean establishments or enjoy a game of tennis at the rather novel Rex Tennis Restaurant, followed by a drink and snack in the grounds of the adjacent Revolutionary Museum contemplating, of all things, Russian antiaircraft guns and captured American tanks and a helicopter left over from the "liberation" of 1975.

The unique Saigon Floating Hotel, shipped up from Australia's Great Barrier

Reef, was the first foreign-owned establishment to begin catering to the hordes of business travelers pouring into Vietnam. It's been joined by the neoclassic Century Hotel and, in Hanoi, the elegant, newly renovated Pullman Metropole. This international-class competition has forced some of the traditional hotels to upgrade their decor and service — establishments like the Rex, Caravelle (now the Doc Lap Hotel) and re-nowned Hotel Continental in downtown

Saigon, which has unfortunately turned its famous open patio bar, a popular haunt for correspondents during the war, into a closed, icily air-conditioned Italian restaurant and completely ruined one of Asia's best watering holes.

The return of nightlife and entertainment has brought Vietnam's contemporary culture out of the closet. Rock bands and teams of singers are now back on the stage at places like the Palace in Hanoi and Queen Bee in Saigon, and the country's two key cultural centers, the municipal opera houses in both cities, offer everything from piano recitals to heavy metal rock performances to packed audiences almost every evening.

All in all, the Vietnamese are beginning to enjoy life again. It may be happening against a social backdrop that's still stark with poverty, chronic unemployment and the beggars, amputees and homeless street gangs that the war and subsequent social upheaval left in their wake — but the new flowering is definitely there.

Both Laos and Cambodia have followed Vietnam's lead and opened up their economies, with Laos launching the same sort of campaign for foreign investment in 1987. But where Vietnam's development has been shackled since then by the United States

trade and investment embargo, Laos was given Washington's blessing the moment it opened its doors and has been receiving Asian Development Bank (ADB) loans for several years. In fact, foreign aid is estimated to make up more than three-quarters of the national budget.

As in Vietnam, the lifting of restrictions on private enterprise in Laos has led to a virtual counter-revolution. Vientiane is back in business, bustling the way it was when it was the key base for United States-sponsored military activity in the war years. A whole new retail industry is flourishing right throughout the city, ranging from small supermarkets and arts and crafts stores along the main thoroughfare, Thanon Samsenthai, to a new barn-like series of buildings, packed with jewelry, wristwatch, consumer electronics and household products shops, on the site of the old Morning Market. Old hotels like the former French-operated Constellation, now called the Asian Pavilion, and the Lan Xang, Anou and River View, have been tarted up to cater for incoming business travelers and tourists. Elegant new establishments like the Lani Guesthouse and Parasol de Blanc have opened to capture the more up-market visitors and locally based UNESCO officials. New restaurants—the French/Continental Nam Phu and nearby Italian establishment, L'Opera, to name just a couple of them — have brought the city's reputation for fine cuisine back up to scratch.

Like the Vietnamese, the Laos are enjoying life again, encouraged by the relatively benign regime that the Pathet Lao imposed in 1975. While thousands of Vietnamese are reported to have disappeared into re-education camps and other forms of detention after the communist victory, the Laotian revolutionary regime allowed its most hardline, top-level political opponents to "escape" the country, literally turning a blind eye at the Mekong River border as they crossed into Thailand. Though other dissidents certainly suffered, the main communist reprisal seems to have been against the king, Savang Vatthana, and his queen, who refused to cooperate with the revolutionaries and hadn't been heard of since 1977 when it was announced they were being

committed to a re-education center somewhere in the north. It has since been announced that they died.

The years of isolation and social "restructuring" have had a deep effect on the country and its capital. Where Vientiane was once notorious for its brothels, vice clubs like the infamous White Rose and the astonishing range of marijuana offered openly for sale on stalls in the old Morning Market, the city and its society are now virtually squeaky clean. Of all the "new" Indo-Chinese, the Laos are probably the most

reserved — not unfriendly, by any means, but less inclined than the Vietnamese and Cambodians to get overtly excited and familiar with foreigners. In some ways this is easier for visitors to deal with: although you're definitely a tourist, you can move through Laos feeling that you're part of the society and not the center of attention.

The most spontaneously friendly and hospitable people of Indo-China are the Cambodians, which is fascinating when you consider the horrors that they've been through. It's just as intriguing to examine the reasons why they should greet visitors

OPPOSITE and ABOVE: The motorbike and bicycle remain Vietnam's main form of personal transportation as the country tries to modernize.

with such exuberance. The virtual destruction of the country's middle class led to mostly rural people flooding into Phnom Penh when it was repopulated after the Vietnamese invasion. They brought a charming curiosity and lack of sophistication with them, and this has reinvigorated a city which was once cynically cosmopolitan.

Foreigners, particularly the United Nations personnel, are also their first line of protection against the Khmer Rouge; and this is another obvious reason why they welcome visitors so heartily. At the time of writ-

ing, the United Nations troops were still playing a largely unarmed non-combat role, more preoccupied with civil and political reconstruction than military action against the entrenched guerrillas. The lack of weaponry had made it infinitely easier for both communities to cooperate and enjoy each other's company. On the one side, I found that most Cambodians not only welcome but respect the United Nations presence; on the other, I met many United Nations soldiers who'd fallen in love with the country and its people and were trying to extend their three-month tours of duty.

ABOVE: Cyclo driver and typical load, Danang.
OPPOSITE: Cambodian student, Phnom Penh.

It goes without saying that the fear that people in the southern "government" zones have of the Khmer Rouge should not be underestimated. Every Cambodian I spoke with in Phnom Penh was convinced that if the guerrillas were allowed to take over the country, the killings would happen again. In fact, the murders haven't stopped: insisting, against all evidence, that Vietnamese forces are still operating in Cambodia, the Khmer Rouge have been massacring whole families and even villages of ethnic Vietnamese who've lived in Cambodia for years. More ominous is the prospect that, having once wiped out Cambodia's capitalist class, they'll turn their guns on a completely new generation of entrepreneurs that's sprung up in Phnom Penh and other major centers since the United Nations moved in.

The United Nations presence, aimed at building a new, democratic society, has given Cambodia the most liberal business and investment base in Indo-China. Just catering for thousands of United Nations personnel has also meant a radical transformation of this previously impoverished, ruined society. Phnom Penh and other major cities are flooded with consumer imports; bars and restaurants are opening as fast as the seed-money, most of it from Hong Kong and Thailand, hits the local banks; new hotels, ranging from the deluxe Cambodiana and Phnom Penh Floating Hotel to modest guesthouses, are opening up all over the place — many of the down-market establishments cashing in on the chronic shortage of United Nations accommodation.

This sudden surge of development has given Phnom Penh the look of chaos and near-anarchy that Saigon had in the early build-up days of the Vietnam War. The trappings of new wealth are blossoming in an urban setting that's probably the most derelict of all the cities of Indo-China — its old French commercial and civic architecture crumbling away, most of its streets badly broken and potholed. At peak times, the traffic is incredible — a turbulent tangle of Land Cruisers, trucks, ramshackle buses and thousands upon thousands of bicycles, motorbikes and pedal-cyclos all

doing their best to avoid any semblance of order.

But that's what gives Phnom Penh its special character, and the same could be said for Hanoi, Saigon, Vientiane and most of the other cities and large towns of Indo-China. The whole region and its people are in a state of upheaval and transition. The energy, vibrancy and exoticism of Indo-China are flourishing once again. But the time-warp that it's languished in for nearly two decades hasn't yet completely given way. It is still a place of history, waiting for the future to unfold.

turing boom that's taken place in China's southern special economic zone.

If there's any question about the region's future, it's just who is going to lead this dramatic economic renaissance. In this respect, history is repeating itself: Vietnam, flexing potentially powerful economic and political muscle, sees itself as the dominant partner in a new Indo-China economic zone; but to the west, the Thais are again claiming cultural and economic suzerainty over Laos and Cambodia. And the outcome of this struggle may well hinge on

THE ECONOMY

With Vietnam at its fore, Indo-China is standing on the threshold of an economic boom. The region is rich in agricultural, marine, forestry and mineral resources, and war and austerity have kept all these treasures intact. It has a huge pool of educated but cheap labor ready to offer highly competitive offshore manufacturing for the established export economies of Asia and elsewhere. It's hungry for consumer goods, and for investment funds to build an industrial base and redevelop its neglected infrastructure. It sees itself as a future Pearl River Delta, copying the phenomenal manufac-

what happens in Cambodia in the coming years.

In the meantime, Vietnam's plans for economic development can be taken as a blueprint for the entire region. Offering some of the most attractive investment regulations of any developing socialist nation — including 100 percent foreign ownership of selected enterprises — it has charted a course which it hopes will bring it to economic "takeoff" by the year 2000. By then, it would be sustaining an annual growth of seven to eight percent and a per capita income of around US$500 and be ready to graduate to NIE (Newly Industrialized Economy) status.

Hanoi's economic architects, led by experienced southerners, see tourism development as the first step, bringing in much-needed foreign exchange. Then the "transformation industries" — foreign joint- venture manufacturing based on textiles, electronics and other export products — would take over, creating an industrial base. Agricultural production would be boosted and modernized, and it's this sector which is most vividly reflecting the country's enormous economic potential. With the introduction of free enterprise and the removal of barriers to the flow of produce between provinces and cities, Vietnam has

But the biggest drawback to Vietnam's development continues to be its decrepit infrastructure — roads, bridges, ports, airports, transportation and communications. It needs massive international financing for repair and modernization, but has been denied it by the United States embargo and Washington's dominance of the World Bank, IMF and Asian Development Bank. By early 1993, it appeared that this key stumbling block was about to be removed. Washington and Hanoi seemed to be ready to settle the MIA (missing United States

already progressed from a food-deficient nation to the world's third largest exporter of rice.

Much of its hopes are pinned on oil production from a series of former Soviet-operated offshore leases in the Gulf of Tonkin and the South China Sea off central and southern Vietnam. Now transferred to some of the world's leading multinationals, including BP Petroleum, these fields produced four million barrels of crude in 1991 and the plan is to top 10 million barrels a year by the end of this decade. No major new strikes had been made at the time of writing, but the feeling among foreign executives was that the southern fields, in particular, could prove to be a new North Sea.

servicemen) issue, American businessmen were being allowed to negotiate, but not activate, deals in Vietnam, Japan had lifted its own ban on loans and financial aid and there was hope that one of the first moves of the new Clinton administration would be to accelerate normalization.

For all this, Vietnam is most definitely viewed as the new frontier of business and investment in Asia. As one Western oil executive in Saigon told me: "We see tremendous potential here, and probably better prospects than those in other countries of the region, including Thailand."

OPPOSITE: Fishermen repair nets on Vietnam's Nha Trang beach. ABOVE: New fishing trawlers are being built as the economy revives.

This is undoubtedly worrying the Thais — the specter of a powerful new economic force challenging Bangkok's pivotal strategy in Southeast Asia. Thai traders and investors have flooded into Laos and Cambodia, swiftly nailing up their shingles before Vietnam is strong enough to move in. Thai money has gone initially into hotels, restaurants, bars and small manufacturing industries in Vientiane and Phnom Penh. But it has also been directed at one particular industry which has embroiled Bangkok in a potentially bitter political and environmental controversy — logging.

Both Laos and Cambodia are mainly agricultural economies, though they also possess extensive mineral deposits which require heavy investment to exploit. In the short-term, both are selling off the one resource that can be easily extracted — timber — and the Thais, having already created an environmental crisis with their own wholesale deforestation, have virtually seized upon this opportunity as their own.

Laos is particularly vulnerable — only 10 percent of its land is arable, the rest is forest. The construction of a bridge across the Mekong at Nong Khai, donated by Australia and opened in 1993, is seen by some environmentalist and economists as not just the country's first real physical link with the outside world, but an opportunity for increased Thai exploitation as well.

In Cambodia, Thai logging operations have taken a more cynical and sinister twist — creating a business partnership with the Khmer Rouge. It's from the Khmer Rouge territories, close to the Thai border, that most of the teak and other valuable timbers are being extracted. It's not just causing environmental concern, the possible unchecked rape of Cambodia's remaining forests, it's also triggered a political crisis. The Thai relationship with the Khmer Rouge goes beyond business deals: the Darth Vader of the guerrilla movement, Pol Pot, is reported to have been living for some time in safe exile in a Thai military camp close to the border. Diplomatic efforts have been made to sever this nefarious partnership, with United Nations pressure to close the Thai border crossings and stop the logging and France condemning what it terms

a "criminal" situation, but it remains just one of the issues which is endangering Cambodia's future in the "new" Indo-China.

POLITICS

If you talk to some of the thousands of Vietnamese boat people still seeking refugee status in the camps of Hong Kong, Malaysia and the Philippines, they'll tell you that the dramatic economic changes in Vietnam are all very well — but what about political reform? And in some respects they have a valid point.

Vietnam is still a socialist country, its people still forced to toe the Communist Party line, its economy still centrally controlled. It has opened its doors, but at the higher echelons of government it remains suspicious of foreign activities and motives. Its security apparatus is still so tight that foreigners can rarely visit a private Vietnamese home without the local police getting there first. Tourists and even locally based foreign business people cannot visit some provinces and cities without special permits; visiting media are kept under tight control, and photographers and TV crews require customs permission to take film and video out of the country. Political change is dragging its feet in the wake of economic liberalization — yet change is certainly taking place.

The open door policy of 1986 came about because a liberal southerner, Nguyen Van Linh, assumed power at the Sixth Congress of the Communist Party. Once the door was opened, once the fundamental decision to bring back free enterprise was made, it would have taken a reactionary crackdown similar to China's Tiananmen Square massacre — especially in the south — to turn the clock of change back to where it was.

The switch to a market economy has meant that a whole gamut of laws and regulations has had to be rewritten, and new ones made, particularly in that anathema of the communist state, property ownership. The influx of foreign investment has meant the liberalization of banking laws, allowing private and joint-venture banks to compete with the previous monopoly of official institutions. The search for export markets has meant that Vietnamese are now allowed to travel overseas. Thousands of detainees have been released from re-education camps and some prominent intellectuals and former capitalist rehabilitated as the state casts about for people capable of guiding and managing economic reconstruction. Moreover, the state itself has had to change. Immediate decision-making power is said to have switched from the unwieldy Communist Party politburo to a smaller and more decisive executive council, with each member responsible for a particular arm of government and administration. According to one Saigon-based foreign political observer, the trend seems to be toward "the Westminster system, with ministers responsible for portfolios — but this could take quite some time to happen."

Another trend has been presented by one of the leading figures involved in the reform program, a prominent Saigon business consultant and former Deputy Prime Minister of the wartime South Vietnam. "What we're aiming for is market socialism," he says, "a free-market economy and society with firm, but not dictatorial, guidance and leadership from the top. We really don't think that Western-style moral democracy suits Vietnam at the present time. We've seen how South Korea and Singapore achieved spectacular economic growth, both of them under firm leadership, and we feel this is what Vietnam needs to accomplish its prime task — to catch up and compete effectively with the rest of the world."

Whatever, there are two other clear trends that point to comparatively radical political change in the future. The demand for talented, foreign-trained technocrats to run the economic program means that power will ultimately shift from the surviving old guard of wartime revolutionaries. And it remains to be seen how long the Vietnamese will be content with the power to conduct their own business affairs but otherwise not think for themselves.

In Laos, the death of President Kaysone Phomvihane in November 1992 seemed to herald the same passing of the communist old guard in favor of younger, more liberal blood. However, his successor, Nouhak

Phoumsavan, is a similarly hard-line communist and ally of Vietnam, underscoring the snail's pace of change in Laos and Hanoi's struggle to maintain its political grip on the country in the face of economic incursions by the Thais.

But while Phoumsavan's accession maintains the supreme power of the Lao People's Revolutionary Party, or communist party, governing through its politburo and Central Committee, an undercurrent of economic reforms similar to those in Vietnam has served notice of the course the

country will no doubt take in the future. The first legal code since the revolution was enacted in 1988, establishing a Western-style system of courts and justice, along with liberal investment laws. In 1990, Laos was given its first official constitution since the Pathet Lao victory. It not only ratifies the principle of free enterprise but also removes the term socialism and the hammer and sickle from the nation's political banner.

The Lao government is regarded as one of the most secretive in the world. Access to its 12 ministries is not easy for outsiders, and media publicity is rare. But it is known that Laos shares Vietnam's prime problem — finding the experience and talent needed to build and manage a modern economy. Otherwise, there's hardly any overt evidence of repression or interference in everyday Lao life; in fact, the society appears to be the most serene and idyllic in Asia. There seems to be complete religious freedom in this devoutly Buddhist domain, and when you witness

ABOVE: Poster in Hue recalls Vietnam's post-war revolutionary era.

the passion with which the Laos celebrate their Buddhist festivals the term "Buddhist socialism" springs to mind. You can't help speculating that this is one popular power that the Lao communists, at least, prudently came to terms with, instead of trying to conquer.

The same cannot be said, of course, of the Khmer Rouge in Cambodia. During their four-year rampage they destroyed Buddhist temples, murdered monks and virtually eliminated all social and political institutions in their crazed vision of a new agrarian

society which, if it had been Europe, would have turned the clock back to the darkest of medieval times. Much of Cambodian society has had to be completely reconstructed — and this promises, ironically, to give Cambodia the most liberal political character in the region.

Where Vietnam and Laos are resisting democratic reform, it has been the linchpin of United Nations efforts to rebuild Cambodia's society. It's not just the political framework that's had to be restored — just about everything from public security to social services has had to be built virtually from

ABOVE and OPPOSITE: Buddhism has survived the Marxist revolution in Laos, proving to be a powerful cohesive force.

the ground up. But it's in the political sphere that the most dramatic reforms have taken place. Since the mid-1993 elections and their crucial significance for Cambodia's redevelopment, more than a dozen political parties representing liberals, conservatives, pressure groups and Buddhists are jostling for a place in the new political order. Of the three main rebel factions, the Khmer Rouge did not field candidates. As the election approached, the Khmer Rouge refused to take part, presenting the United Nations and the country with a grave dilemma.

A kingdom has been established under Sihanouk, nominally a constitutional monarchy but in which he may well forget the word "constitutional", unless some remarkable change has overtaken him; his two sons have squabbled over the extent of their own influence, and one is now prime minister. But Sihanouk, always a catalyst in any political shift in his long-suffering country, is an old man after 40 years of political skulduggery, and also unwell. Cambodia's future is far from certain, and in spite of prattle about how " the world will never tolerate a return to Khmer Rouge power," the sad truth is that the world will tolerate anything at all that suits it at the time.

RELIGION

When China launched its open door policy a while after Mao's death, following over 20 years of hare-brained social and economic engineering, it got to work immediately rebuilding and renovating damaged temples. It wasn't just the restoration of religious freedom that was behind it — more the need to give tourists something to see. Then the monks and worshipers had to be allowed back to give an air of authenticity. I'm not saying that this cynicism has governed all religious restoration, but it is undeniable that tourism development and the demand for exoticism is playing a major role in the revival of traditional culture right through the socialist world.

In Indo-China, the revival has been more popular, more spirited, reflecting the fact that communities like southern Vietnam, Laos and Cambodia have been under communist

discipline for a comparatively shorter period. While it's true to say that for every Buddhist or Catholic priest there is a party cadre keeping tabs on the congregation, there's been a wholesale rush back to the images and altars that puts Indo-China's socialist experiment into proper perspective — a slight deviation along a well-trodden cultural path that stretches back many centuries.

We've read how Hinduism was a major spiritual force in Indo-China, with the region's two greatest kingdoms, Champa and Angkor profoundly affected by the cult of the devaraja, or god-king, in which the ruler acquired divine status. The Viets brought Confucianism from China — notwithstanding Confucius' mutterings about them — and this, together with Taosim, percolated down from the north. Confucianism is more a system for the ordering of social responsibilities and relationships than a religion, while Taoism concerns itself with the individual's harmony with nature. In the second century, a new spiritual influence, Buddhism, began sweeping the region, making its way from India through China to the Red River Delta and then down through the kingdom of the Chams. It eventually became the dominant faith in Indo-China, adopted as the state religion by the Ly Dynasty in north Vietnam in the years 1010 to 1225, and spreading from there.

Although it came under Confucian counter-attack in later years, Buddhism prevailed by coming to terms with other faiths around it — most notably, Taoism and Hinduism. One of the region's most precious religious sites, the ruins of Wat Phu near Pakse in southern Laos, is regarded as the first Buddhist temple in Southeast Asia. Yet its architecture is distinctly Khmer Hindu, reflecting the marriage that Buddhism was able to secure with the monuments of original faiths. The great Hindu city and temples of Angkor had likewise switched their religious focus from mainstream Hinduism to a form of Buddhism by the thirteenth century.

The arrival of French and other European missionaries brought Roman Catholicism to the region, and this also eventually flourished — strengthened and promoted by colonial rule, especially among the more

cosmopolitan, urban Indo-Chinese. If you look at the general religious profile of Indo-China today it is surviving outcrops of Christianity — some of the most beautiful old churches and cathedrals you can imagine — in a great sea of Buddhism, with Chinese, Hindu and Muslim temples here and there, most erected by immigrant traders who flocked to the region during the reign of the French.

While Catholicism and Buddhism have managed to get on quite harmoniously with each other, their relationship hasn't been

without its upheavals. When Ho Chi Minh's communists gained power in North Vietnam in 1954, nearly one million Vietnamese Catholics fled to the south. There they established a Catholic, anti-communist oligarchy headed by Ngo Dinh Diem and successive presidents and supported by the Roman Catholic church in the United States. Their power, not to mention the corruption and favoritism that marked the wartime regimes, provoked and alienated the Buddhist majority in the south, triggered strikes and student unrest and led to the horrifying,

OPPOSITE: Sacred white elephant is paraded through Vientiane during That Luang festival.
ABOVE: Huge firecrackers at festival in Dong Ky, Vietnam.

internationally publicized self-immolations by Buddhist monks that led to Diem's downfall.

Not surprisingly, Catholicism came firmly under the official thumb in Vietnam after 1975. Many churches were closed and congregations intimidated. But a general restoration of religious freedom has taken place since the moves to liberalize the society began. And it's progressed quite rapidly. On my first return to Saigon in December 1991, I attempted to film a morning Mass in the beautiful Notre Dame Cathedral in Saigon. The priest begged me not to, explaining that it would cause trouble with the authorities. Six months later, on a second visit, I filmed in there quite freely, and no-one turned a hair.

Right through Vietnam, the old churches and cathedrals are now filled with worshipers each Mass — Saigon's Notre Dame, the striking, almost medieval St Joseph Cathedral in Hanoi, the beautiful domed Notre Dame Cathedral in Hue, just to name a few. But when you take into account that only about eight percent of Vietnam's population is Christian, the revival of Buddhism and other beliefs is far more dramatic. Prayers, joss and ritual offerings are an everyday scene again at Taoist and Buddhist temples and shrines in all the major Vietnamese cities — places like the Tran Quoc and Quan Thanh temples around Hanoi's West Lake; the revered Thien Mu pagoda and temple overlooking the Perfume River in Hue; and two particularly evocative temples in Saigon, the tiny but elaborate Chinese Thien Hau Pagoda in Cholon, dedicated to the Goddess of the Sea, and the Le Van Duyet Temple three kilometers from the downtown area.

But nowhere in Indo-China is Buddhism still celebrated with such color and fervor than in Laos, where the faith seems to have stood as a social bulwark against the excesses of Marxism. The great temples of Vientiane and Luang Prabang — and there are literally dozens of them — are flourishing again, apparently undamaged by the communist reign; and some are being renovated to cash in on a growing tourist trade. In fact, the only damage seems to have been committed in the war years before the

revolution — priceless images and relics stolen from them by United States and other foreign correspondents, servicemen and art dealers.

The extent to which Buddhism has triumphed in Laos can be witnessed at two major festivals each year. In November, thousands of monks and novices flock to Vientiane to join the population in a tumultuous three-day celebration centered on the country's most important Buddhist monument, the towering Pha That Luang (Great Sacred Stupa) and monastery on the city's

northeastern fringe. In April, elephant processions highlight the three-day lunar new year festival in Luang Prabang.

In Cambodia, Buddhism and other faiths are emerging from a period of wanton destruction waged by the Khmer Rouge. Christian churches were completely destroyed during their rampage, and one of the country's most sacred Buddhist monuments, the hilltop temples and mosque of Udong, 40 km (25 miles) north of the capital, bears evidence of the suppression — the two main temples are in virtual ruins, along with huge reclining and sitting Buddha images which were dynamited by the revolutionaries. For all this, much of the country's Buddhist heritage is reasonably intact —

most notably, the elaborate Royal Palace in Phnom Penh, a complex of halls and temples fashioned in the style of the Grand Palace in Bangkok, which the Khmer Rouge are said to have preserved in an effort to bolster their international image.

Of all the religions of Indo-China, one bears special mention for its unique color and ritual — the Cao Dai of southern Vietnam. Based in Tay Ninh, northwest of Saigon on the Cambodian border, Cao Dai has a priesthood modeled on that of the Roman Catholic Church and a doctrine

and the almost medieval costumes of priests, cardinals and other clergy, the Cao Dai have become one of the region's biggest tourist drawcards.

MUSIC AND DANCE

One thing that I found fascinating in Vietnam is the unique and quite bizarre range of musical instruments that's emerged from the shadows of war. In the north, much of the style of traditional music and dance can

which borrows much from Mahayana Buddhism but otherwise combines beliefs from all the world's major religions. It was founded in 1926 by a Vietnamese civil servant, Ngo Minh Chieu, and most of its early followers were Vietnamese bureaucrats working in the French administration.

The Cao Dai virtually ruled Tay Ninh province and parts of the Mekong Delta in their early days, and resisted the communist Viet Cong during the Vietnam War. They came under revolutionary suppression after the war, but are flourishing again today — and you have only to visit their ornate Great Temple in Tay Ninh to realize why. With Masses celebrated four times a day, the vast congregations resplendent in white robes

be traced back to early Chinese influence, with a similar five-note pentatonic scale and orchestras of up to 40 musicians playing the sort of instruments you'd see in China.

But the moody, melodic base of Vietnamese music is provided by an instrument which is very much their own — the danbau, a single-string zither with a willowy tuning rod at one end which, caressed by the musician's fingers, controls the tone and pitch of each note. Aside from reed flutes, gongs and mandolin-type stringed instruments, they also play a bamboo xylophone which hangs like a curtain before

OPPOSITE and ABOVE: Traditional court dance and young dancers at Thai Hoa Palace in Hue.

the musician. Then there's another bamboo instrument for base accompaniment in which the hands are clapped at the mouths of thick, graduated tubes very much like the pipes of an organ — the action producing pulses of air which provide a series of low, resonant burps.

These instruments provide the basis of folk, classical, chamber and theatrical music and dance which are being staged again throughout Vietnam, in the municipal opera houses of Hanoi and Saigon, at conservatories and cultural centers and at special cul-

tural shows put on by the leading hotels. One venue of special note is a small auditorium in the central Eden Building in Saigon starring the quite astonishing Phudong Percussion Band, a troupe of jolly troubadours who specialize in ethnic minority music, bursting on to the stage clicking a series of weird wooden instruments that create a frenzied symphony of bullfrogs and cicadas burping and chattering to the accompaniment of drums and gongs.

Elsewhere, Vietnam's cosmopolitan heritage means that Western music — anything from Haydn to heavy metal — is resounding again from the municipal halls, dance clubs and bars. At one end of the spectrum, you can eat to the music of Chopin at the Piano

Bar in Hanoi, or enjoy a student chamber recital in at a conservatory right alongside the Citadel in Hue; and at the other, drop into clubs like The Palace in Hanoi or Queen Bee in Saigon and marvel at the natural rhythm, mimicry and professionalism that the Vietnamese share with the Filipinos when it comes to rock and pop music.

In Laos and Cambodia, the traditional music is more what we would identify as Thai, with horseshoe-shaped gong bands and squeaky hilltribe bamboo flutes more common in recitals and as a dance accompaniment. The dances are more subtle and stylized than those of the Vietnamese, more the elaborately costumed court dances that you see in Bangkok — the dancers themselves heavily brocaded and wearing jeweled headgear, with the movement of the face and hands providing the story and drama of the choreography. Folk dancing in both countries is likewise similar to the hilltribe shows that you may have seen in Thailand's Golden Triangle., Buddhism

At present, the venues are similar to those in Vietnam — mainly the hotels, which stage regular cultural shows with buffets. The new Villa de la Princess hotel in Luang Prabang, for example, features traditional Lao music and dance at least once a week. In Cambodia, the old Aseana Grand Hotel in Siem Reap, close to the Angkor temples, also features local dance troupes, and the highly-regarded National Cambodian Dance Company occasionally stages performances in Angkor Wat itself.

Modern music and dance in both these countries is again strikingly similar to what you'd find in Bangkok. The Thai ramwong, in which couples writhe and sway gently about each other on the dance floor, never touching but using their hands and body movement for intimate expression, is a nightclub favorite in Vientiane and Phnom Penh. Other than that, the entertainment at discos and clubs right across the region reflects the general transition from communist puritanism to the modern rave — dances can be a sedate fox-trot or tango one minute, with the cadres swanning flamboyantly across the floor with their wives, and a writhing, stomping disco rock number the next. With a ramwong or two in between.

ARTS AND CRAFTS

As in China, the socialist revolution stifled or deliberately crushed the cultural refinement of Vietnam, Laos and Cambodia, replacing traditional arts with politically correct propaganda. With no tourists to speak of, traditional handicrafts also went by the board; and this is one social area in which the re-emergence is not so dramatic.

To be completely blunt about it, there's not much to buy anywhere in Indo-China, unless you have a taste for garish lacquer or mother-of-pearl furniture and artifacts in Vietnam, or equally vulgar Chinese-style stoneware, porcelain, marble and glassware which can be found right through the region and which reflect the over-elaborate state that these arts got themselves into in China's last dynastic period, the Qing. Moreover, much of the traditional silverwork and other crafts that you'll find on sale in Laos and Cambodia have actually been imported from Thailand.

Having said that, there are some cultural nuggets which can still be found amid the general kitsch. Vietnam's distinctive porcelain elephants, which literally flooded Western markets during the Vietnam War, are on sale again in craft and souvenir shops in Hanoi and Saigon. They're bulky and heavy, but can be shipped home on the plane with your luggage. Some of the lacquered screens and furniture are also quite attractive, but be warned that Asian rosewood and other exotic materials can dry up and crack in centrally heated Western homes. Other than that, you'll find a lot of Soviet-era Russian watches on sale throughout Vietnam — timepieces celebrating perestroika, the Bush–Gorbachev summit and even the Desert Shield campaign in the Gulf — and these make unusual souvenirs. You'll also undoubtedly come across old Zippo cigarette lighters purportedly left over from the Vietnam War, inscribed with United States names and epitaphs like "I must be going to Heaven, 'cos I've served my time in Hell." Be warned that a lot of these are fakes, turned out in cottage workshops especially for the new foreign invasion.

In Laos, the most interesting folk art on sale is traditional weavings, most of them featuring animist patterns and motifs asso-

ciated with hilltribe arts. The genuine products can be found in a series of craft shops on Vientiane's main street, Thanon Samsenthai, close to the Pavilion Hotel — genuine because they're old and woven from traditional vegetable-dyed threads. Elsewhere, purists point to the modern chemical-dyed materials which are now being used on cottage looms, but a visit to one particularly flourishing new weaving center just outside Luang Prabang will convince you that while the dyes have changed the workmanship and creativity haven't deteriorated.

Vientiane's modernized Central Market has one section devoted to gold and silver jewelry and watches, but nothing that you can't really buy in Bangkok. My tip is to look for Russian watches, costing between US$18 and $20, which are not just souvenirs of the collapsed USSR but feature tanks, submarines and other military reminders of the Cold War.

In Cambodia, the huge domed Central Market in Phnom Penh has a core section full of gold, silver and watches, but elsewhere there's not much available except UNTAC (United Nations Temporary Assistance

OPPOSITE: Ornately carved temple doors in Vientiane. ABOVE: Temple images factory in Phnom Penh.

Command) T-shirts. However, in stores that line the commercial blocks around the market you can find beautifully woven cotton and silk sarongs — many of them interwoven, Thai-style, with silver and gold thread. Indeed, so-called Thai silk is in fact an import of a Cambodian craft. Then there's the most popular souvenir of this ravaged country, which you'll find just about anywhere you go — the distinctive red-, blue- and grey-checkered cotton headscarfs worn by most rural Cambodians and the Khmer Rouge.

CUISINE

The proletarian revolution which followed the war also reduced the cuisines of Vietnam and its neighbors to the level of basic sustenance, which is understandable considering the austerity and social leveling that the communists brought in. However, the return of tourism has revived the region's restaurant industry, and this in turn has put a touch of sophistication and refinement back into the native cuisines.

Vietnamese cuisine has little of the vast breadth and variety of Chinese food, covering probably 500 different dishes compared with some 2,000 in the Chinese culinary compendium. But it's distinctive, all the same, perhaps more delicate and subtle than Chinese food, relying more on natural ingredients than sauces for flavor.

ABOVE: Wedding celebrations, Vung Tau, Vietnam. OPPOSITE TOP: Soft drinks vendor, Nha Trang. BOTTOM: Snack stall, Nha Trang beach.

Spring rolls, minced pork in light pancakes, grilled shrimp on sugar cane and marinated beef slices on prawn crackers are more the style of Vietnamese food, with much use of fresh lettuce and mint leaves as an accompaniment to main dishes. And there are two staples to the cuisine which distance Vietnamese food from its neighbors: the traditional breakfast of steaming *pho*, pronounced "*phar*," a bowl of rice noodles with shredded beef, chicken and pork with fresh chopped shallots, and *nuoc mam*, a condiment of fermented fish essence, which is added to almost all dishes and has a taste which is infinitely more delightful and addictive than one might think.

Lao and Cambodian food, on the other hand, is very similar to Thai: menus in both countries rely on fiery green and red chilies as an ingredient and condiment. Fish, chicken, pork and dried beef are added to rice and noodles, and where the Thai cuisine is noted for beef and chicken salads liberally boosted with green chilies, the Laos and Cambodians have a zesty version in which meats, fish or vegetables are spiced with garlic, green onions and lime juice.

The large ethnic Chinese populations in all three countries mean that the Chinese cuisine stands staunchly alongside native food, and there are many Chinese restaurants in all major cities. And they share something else with their giant neighbor, an enthusiastic but questionable taste for exotic wildlife: bears, deer, civet cats, snakes, rice birds and the pangolin, or long-nosed scaly anteater. The Lan Xang Hotel in Vientiane has a riverside restaurant with the unlikely name of **Sukiyaki** which serves braised scaly anteater and another exotic but obviously confused preparation of venison called "bleeding moose."

Japanese restaurants have sprung up in all major centers, catering for an influx of Japanese traders and executives who've been flooding all three countries with motorbikes, cars and trucks and electronic goods to capture the market before the United States embargo lifts. You'll find Korean restaurants in most cities, too. In Vientiane and Phnom Penh, many of the top restaurants are owned by Thais, and a lot of them serve not Thai but quality Western

or Continental food. The Thai-owned **La Paillote**, opposite the Central Market in Phnom Penh, is one of the best Continental restaurants in the region, packed each evening with United Nations officers and Western expatriates. When I was there it had a sign on the door pleading with guests not to smoke marijuana on the premises.

The French cuisine is also undergoing a renaissance of sorts, with the international-class hotels such as the opulent Pullman Metropole in Hanoi leading the revival. But one French tradition that the Indo-Chinese have never lost their taste for is fresh, crisply baked bread, or baguettes, and in all cities and large towns right across the region you'll find stalls laden with them each morning. It's one of the great delights of Indo-China today to breakfast or lunch on baguettes filled with thick slices of French-style ham, pate and cheese with rich, creamy café filtre. It's another delight altogether to experience Indo-Chinese coffee. Although freeze-dried Nescafé is flooding the region — considered to be quite the modern thing to offer — you can still get the traditional beverage in most cafes and restaurants. It's locally grown coffee filtered onto an inch or so of sweetened condensed milk, then stirred into a mixture which has the color and texture of paddy mud. It's unusual, but it provides a deliciously powerful kick-start to any day.

GEOGRAPHY AND CLIMATE

Indo-China is a beautiful region, and one of many remarkable physical contrasts. A fleeting overview would compare the dramatic offshore karst, or limestone, formations of Halong Bay, north of Hanoi, with the vast, dazzling sweep of flooded rice-plains in the Mekong Delta, the crumpled, green-swaddled folds and sharp peaks of the mountains of Laos with the tranquil surrealism of Cambodia's southern ricelands — flat green pastures with tall sugar palms poking up like giant lollipops here and there.

Each country has its own contrasts. Vietnam, stretching more than 1,600 km (990 miles) down the eastern seaboard of Indo-China,

is virtually two huge rice-plains — the north Red River and southern Mekong deltas — connected by a spine of jungled mountains, the Annamite Cordillera, which forms the Central Highlands. Within this general physical profile, other distinctions appear: long swathes of sanded, untouched beaches which stretch one after the other from north to south; the pristine coastal bays and flat rice fields of the region between Danang and Hue, set against the rising foothills and high mountain passes of the Central Highlands; the largely arid central region of the country,

beyond Quang Tri and what used to be the Demilitarized Zone, compared with the lush riverine landscape and rich farming hamlets that lead into the delta area south of Saigon.

Laos is far more rugged, with nearly three-quarters of its landlocked terrain covered with mountains and plateaus, networked with rivers that rush west to the Mekong. Some of the hills are more than 2,000 m (6,500 ft) high in Xieng Khwang province, home of the Plain of Jars. In stark contrast, the Mekong River Valley around Vientiane and Savannakhet is a flat, fertile plain and the source of most of the country's food. The mood of the landscape changes dramatically between Vientiane and the upland regions — sultry farm lands, dotted with palms, on the one hand, and a harsh, somewhat bleak red-soiled terrain that's reminiscent of outback Australia in the Xieng Khwang area.

Cambodia is basically a broad central alluvial plain, densely populated and fed by the Mekong River, with hills, mountain ranges and escarpments to its southwest, north and east. The Mekong Delta begins in this central region, and the river is several kilometers wide in some areas. It splits into two separate courses, the Mekong itself and

in the 8°C to 15°C range. It can get particularly cold in the Lao mountains, especially on the Xieng Kwang plateau and the Plain of Jars. Otherwise, there are really only two seasons to Indo-China: hot and wet and hot and dry. In the summer, Hanoi gets extremely hot and humid, with temperatures often above 30°C, and the heat intensifies as you go south. The southern monsoon brings a great deal of rain, but it's a fairly benign season. In Viêtnam, Laos and Cambodia you generally get one refreshing cloudburst a day, usually in the late afternoon, with fine

the Bassac River, at Phnom Penh before sprawling eastward into southern Vietnam. Forests cover the Eastern Highlands and hills in the southwest, close to the Thai border, where the Khmer Rouge have been operating their lucrative lumber trade with the Thais. The southern coast, facing the Gulf of Thailand, is the country's future tourism drawcard, a potential resort playground of sandy palm-fringed beaches and islands that look like tropical atolls from the air.

Although the region lies in the sub-tropical zone, the climate has its own distinct variations. The northern areas of Vietnam and Laos catch the northern monsoons from China and Central Asia in the winter, bringing cold and wet weather and temperatures

weather either side of it. However, Vietnam lies at the end of the path of the Asia-Pacific typhoons, which often dash themselves along its central and northern coasts in the summer months bringing powerful gales, torrential rain and flooding.

The dry season, from October to February, is the best time to travel through the region. The days are warm to hot and the nights cool, though you can get an occasional day of chilly fog and rain. Whatever the season, heat and the risk of dehydration — especially if you travel around on motorbikes or open cyclos — is something that should be kept in mind at all times.

ABOVE: Open-air cafe on the Mekong River in Vientiane — an excellent spot for viewing sunsets.

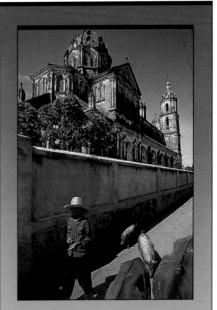

Vietnam:
the North

NORTH VIETNAM holds a special fascination for visitors to Indo-China — a forbidden citadel throughout the Vietnam War and the years of isolation that followed. For decades it was a society that most people could visit only in the imagination, piecing together sketchy media images and accounts of revolutionary rallies, United States bombing statistics, peasant work units rebuilding bridges and dams, human ants struggling in their thousands along the jungled supply lines of the Ho Chi Minh Trail. And Ho Chi Minh himself, his wispy, bearded features symbolizing the stubborn heroism of a society which is only now showing what it actually cost to win the war.

What it cost was progress. Aside from some uninspiring Soviet-era construction — mainly banks and other public buildings — development throughout the north has stood still for more than 40 years, leaving the society to muddle through with an antiquated infrastructure left behind by the French. The north is poorer and more rustic than the south, its industrial capacity comparatively ramshackle, its roads in chronic disrepair, its bridges barely able to handle today's traffic, let alone what's likely to come as the region modernizes.

On the one hand, this predominantly agricultural society illustrates the futility of the Vietnam War — how fundamentally reckless it was to wage a high-tech bombing campaign against rural roads, dikes, bridges, grain storage facilities and rail-lines that could be bandaged back together as fast as they were damaged. But what's more illuminating is the social character of the north — so disciplined, dignified and yet so hospitable, whether urban or rural — and what a tragically wide gulf existed between these people and the vulgar Texan bravado that characterized President Lyndon B. Johnson's ill-fated obsession with bringing them to heel. And as I've mentioned before, there's a rustic, historical charm to the north that the war and isolation have left in their wake — an architecture that's languished in a time-warp since 1945, a cultural naivete that's somewhat refreshing amid the increasingly hard-nosed growth-driven economies of East Asia.

There's already a well-worn tourist route between Hanoi, Haiphong and beautiful Halong Bay, but very little access to the rest of north Vietnam. Although some particularly impoverished areas are still closed to foreigners, the restrictions have more to do with the infrastructure than official security. Poor roads, inadequate accommodation and the rugged, nature of the mountainous provinces bordering China and Laos mean that most travel is restricted to Hanoi and the Red River Delta.

However, with Vietnam's normalization with China and the burgeoning trade between them, it's almost certain that the north's two key railway lines linking Hanoi with the capital of Yunnan Province, Kunming, and Nanning, in Guangxi, will be modernized. And this would open up tourism around Dong Bang on the western border, where a flourishing trading conduit already exists, and hilltribe areas in the northeast where Vietnam melds into the tribal domain that stretches through Yunnan province into northern Laos, Thailand's Golden Triangle and eastern Burma.

Hanoi: Tran Vo Temple OPPOSITE and Buddhist temple keeper ABOVE.

HANOI

One thing that astonishes any visitor to Hanoi is the extent to which the capital's French colonial heritage survived the Vietnam war. Most of it is neglected and crumbling, to be sure, but in the summer months particularly, when the city's tree-lined boulevards are in full leaf, it gives Hanoi an exotic, early European character which you'll not find anywhere else in Vietnam. A series of inner-city lakes and small parks, and its location on the Red River, add to its rustic beauty.

Although densely populated, Hanoi is a relatively small city, its streets laid out in a fairly simple grid created by its French planners; and its four principal lakes are convenient reference points for its various districts. To the north, Hoan Kiem Lake is on the edge of the Old Quarter and the city's main market area around Silk Street and Dong Xuan Market. As you continue northwest to beautiful West Lake (Ho Tay), you pass by the finest surviving examples of the colonial culture — streets full of old French villas, along with St. Joseph Cathedral — and the contrasting neo-socialist monument and vast square of the Ho Chi Minh Mausoleum.

To the south, Thien Quang and Bay Mau lakes are the center of the city's "new" business district, where foreign and local companies are clustering their offices in renovated commercial blocks and villas. From a tourist's point of view, the city's key thoroughfares are Ha Bai Trung Street, running east-west, which has become a venue for imported consumer electronics; Ngo Quyen Street, running north, where you'll find the Pullman Metropole, Bac Nam and Hoa Bien hotels; and Phan Dinh Phung Street which heads northwest from the Old Quarter to West Lake. To the city's northeast, the antique but elegant Long Bien Bridge, built by the French, is one of the city's main cross-river accesses to the international airport and road to Haiphong and Halong Bay; and it's packed most of the day with thousands of rural people flocking in to sell produce and buy supplies in the markets.

WHAT TO SEE

Municipal Theatre
Of all Hanoi's colonial buildings, this is the most centrally located and most splendid, though now showing its age and in considerable need of renovation. Standing at the eastern end of Trang Tien Street on a huge square formed by six intersecting roads, it was built in 1911 as an opera house and is still more commonly referred to as that. The communist takeover of Hanoi on August 16, 1945, was proclaimed from one of its balconies. In 1992 it provided the opening orchestral setting of the French movie *Dien Bien Phu*. Today, the "opera house" and its still-elegant 900-seat auditorium is the cultural

center of Hanoi, packed each night for performances of anything from the Hanoi Symphony Orchestra to operatic recitals, traditional music and dance, Vietnamese pop or Western rock shows.

West Lake (Ho Tay)

Lying on Hanoi's northwestern fringe, West Lake is a tranquil recreational area best viewed at sunset, when the sky and water become a sheet of vivid, changing color. Along the lake's eastern shore, a causeway separates it from a smaller body of water, **Ho Truc Bach** (White Silk Lake), which is also called the "bomb lake." This is where, in October 1967, an American pilot landed after bailing out of his crippled jet, hit by anti-aircraft fire, during an attack on an electronics factory. A

rather crudely sculptured sandstone plaque at the lakeside commemorates the event.

Both West Lake and Truc Bach Lake are now more noted for the open-air restaurants which have resumed business around their shores. On Sundays, particularly, they're packed with wealthier Vietnamese families and are an excellent place in which to mingle and chat with them.

The area also includes two noted temples, the **Tran Quoc and Quan Thanh pagodas**. Tran Quoc, on the eastern shore of West Lake, alongside Thanh Nien Street which runs north between the two lakes, is a fifteenth century temple which was rebuilt in

ABOVE: Hanoi's colonial-era Opera House still flourishes after two wars and a Marxist revolution.

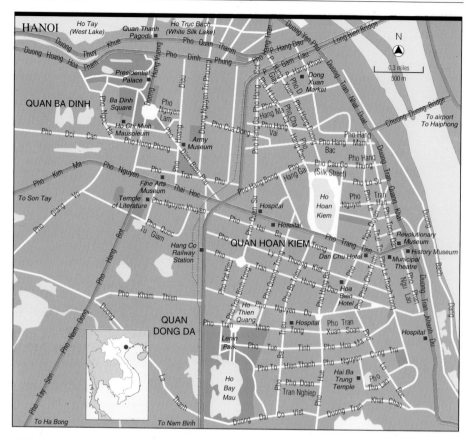

1842. It features a stele believed to have been erected in 1639 which recounts the temple's history, and a main prayer hall and altar decorated with row upon row of Taoist and Buddhist images.

Quan Thanh Pagoda, the more architecturally dramatic of the two, is at the southern end of Thanh Nien Street on Truc Bach Lake. This Ly dynasty (1010–1225) temple has a bronze image and bell dating back to 1677, but what makes it particularly interesting is that its main courtyard is the setting each late afternoon for children's martial arts practice — and another opportunity to relax and chat with local people.

Temple of Literature

You'll find this ancient university and acclaimed example of early Vietnamese architecture about two kilometers west of the city

OPPOSITE: Ngoc Son temple bridge TOP on Hanoi's Hoan Kiem Lake, and entrance to Quan Thanh Pagoda BOTTOM.

center at the intersection of four streets, Nguyen Thai Hoc, Hang Bot, Quoc Tu Giam and Van Mieu. Most of this complex of walled courtyards and pavilions was built in 1070, dedicated to Confucius, and became Vietnam's first university six years later, educating the sons of mandarins. A number of steles, each erected on a stone tortoise, record the names of scholars who were successful in civil service examinations held there from 1442 to 1778. One structure, the Khue Van Pavilion, was built as late as 1802, and the complex underwent repair and renovation in 1920 and 1956.

Hoan Kiem Lake

The tortoise is a divine symbol of Hanoi's central lake, Hoan Kiem, which lies on the edge of the Old Quarter. Right in the center of the lake there's a **small pagoda** commemorating a legend in which a golden tortoise snatched a magical sword which the famed fifteenth century warrior, Emperor Le Loi,

had used to drive the Chinese from north Vietnam. The tortoise disappeared, returning the weapon to the gods, hence the lake's English translation, Lake of the Restored Sword. On the lake's northeastern shore, close to the Silk Street market district, there's another small temple, **Ngoc Son**, reached by a Chinese "willow pattern" wooden bridge called **The Huc** (Rising Sun). Ngoc Son is dedicated to General Tran Hung Dao, who drove the Mongols out in the thirteenth century (and who is commemorated with a towering statue in Saigon's Hero Square);

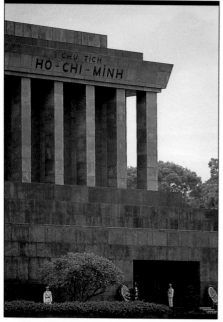

but the temple's main attraction is its bridge and its location — the lake shore alongside it is the venue each morning for public *tai chi* exercises and badminton.

Thien Quang Lake

Lying to the south of Hoan Kiem, this smaller lake is another early morning venue. In fact, it's something of a shock to find such huge crowds in the tree-lined squares and pathways around it — and so early, just after dawn. At the southern end, off Tran Nhan Tong Street, you'll find rows of housewives bending and swaying to the instructions of *tai chi* instructors. Elsewhere, hundreds of children and adults take part in badminton tournaments, keep-fit classes and all sorts

of other sports and pursuits, reflecting the government-imposed social discipline that's been a feature of Hanoi life since the revolution.

One Pillar Pagoda

This delightful wooden structure, set in a lily pond, was built by Emperor Ly Thai Tong (1028–1054) to celebrate a dream in which he was presented with a son and heir by the Goddess of Mercy, Quan The Am Bo Tat. Right after that visitation, he married a young peasant girl who bore him his first son. But the present pagoda isn't the original one — it was rebuilt by the revolutionary government after the French destroyed the original structure in 1954. Today, childless Vietnamese couples pay homage at the shrine, praying for a son. You'll often find young artists there, sketching it from all angles amid the trees. The pagoda's location, off Ong Ich Khiem Street at the southern end of Ba Dinh Square, combines it with a visit to Ho Chi Minh's Mausoleum.

Ho Chi Minh Mausoleum

This towering, marble-clad Soviet-style edifice radiates such power and melancholy that it's a wonder "Uncle Ho" isn't turning in his grave — or in the glass sarcophagus that holds his embalmed corpse. It's known that in his will, Ho ordered that his remains be cremated. Nonetheless, this is still the most revered monument in Vietnam, and Ba Dinh Square, which sprawls before it, the site of annual Kremlin-style victory parades. The whole area is closed to traffic, and on most days the only movement you'll see is a uniformed, armed guard stretching his legs in the trees alongside the mausoleum. Visiting days are Tuesday, Wednesday, Thursday and Saturday from 7:30 am to 11am, and there are obviously a lot of rules to follow — absolutely no photography inside the building; no cameras or bags admitted; no hats; no shorts or tank-tops; no hands in the pockets; no spirited or demonstrative behavior. Each year, Ho's corpse is taken to Moscow for a couple of months — usually September to November — for remedial work to keep it preserved. Close to the mausoleum you'll find Ho's official residence, built in 1958, and the 87-year-old former palace of the

French Governor-General of Indo-China, now the Presidential Palace and used for official receptions.

Museums

There are three museums commemorating Vietnam's struggle against French rule and what is referred to by the Vietnamese as the "American War." The **Army Museum**, situated suitably on Dien Bien Phu Street, features weaponry and scale models depicting Vietnamese victories from the French collapse at Dien Bien Phu to the 1975 fall of

other artifacts explain Vietnamese prehistory, Funan, the Hindu kingdoms of Champa and the Khmers and the country's tumultuous path from dynastic to colonial to communist rule.

The **Fine Arts Museum**, housed in the former French Ministry of Information at 66 Nguyen Thai Hoc Street, close to the Temple of Literature, features some good examples of Vietnamese sculpture, painting, embroidery, lacquerware and other art, but the same people who deified Ho Chi Minh's remains have been at work here too,

Saigon. The **Revolutionary Museum** at 25 Tong Dan Street is no less significant as a national monument, but you really have to have a burning interest in the documentation and faded photographic mementos of Vietnam's emancipation to enjoy it. The **Independence Museum** at 48 Hang Ngang Street is simply the house where Ho Chi Minh drew up Vietnam's Declaration of Independence from French rule in 1945.

You'll find a far more comprehensive view of Vietnamese history at the **History Museum**, located on Phan Ngu Lao Street close to the Municipal Theater. Though as gloomily presented as most museum exhibits in Indo-China, its various displays of pottery, weapons, costumes, models and

turning traditional crafts into a commentary on the communist triumph.

The "Hanoi Hilton"

This sprawling walled bunker off Hai Ba Trung Street was built by the French and is officially known as Hoa Lo Prison. It was, of course, dubbed the Hanoi Hilton by United States POWs — mostly downed pilots — incarcerated there, often after being paraded through the streets, during the Vietnam War. In these more conciliatory times it's something of an embarrassment, and in late 1994 there were reports that it was to be

OPPOSITE: Hanoi's Ho Chi Minh Mausoleum.
ABOVE: Reminders of the apocalypse in the Hanoi War Museum.

pulled down to make way for new commercial development.

Hai Ba Trung Temple

This temple, dedicated to the Trung sisters and their rebellion against the Chinese in 40 AD, isn't on Hai Ba Trung Street — it's about two kilometers to the south of the city center on Tho Lao Street. It features a statue of the two ill-fated sisters kneeling Joan D'Arc-style with raised arms. It will be recalled that after proclaiming themselves queens of the Red River Delta region, they committed suicide rather than surrender to a Chinese counter-attack.

St Joseph Cathedral

Built in 1886, this remarkable square-towered church on Nha Chung Street, west of Hoan Kiem Lake, is a well-weathered shell in an unkempt garden, its stone walls stained and flaked by the elements. But when the light is right, usually in the late afternoon sunshine, it becomes a medieval vision — the effect made all the more profound by the weathering and neglect. It's a photographer's dream. Visitors are quite welcome to take part in Mass, which is held twice a day from 5 to 7 am and 5 to 7 pm. For the rest of the day it's bolted shut, and no matter who you talk to no-one seems to have the key.

Government Guesthouse

This is another photographer's dream, an ornate colonial mansion surrounded by a wrought-iron fence which was once the palace of the French governor. Located on Ngo Quyen Street opposite the Pullman Metropole Hotel, it invites a closer inspection — but at the time of writing it was restricted to official state guests and there was little hope of talking your way beyond the locked gates. Whatever, it stands along with the Pullman Metropole as one of the finest, if one of the few well-preserved, examples of colonial architecture in Hanoi.

The Old Quarter

This teeming rabbit warren of narrow streets and old colonial shop-houses lies north of Hoan Kiem Lake and is the main market district of Hanoi. The chief access to the area

is by way of **Silk Street** (Pho Cau Go) which runs west toward the Red River from a traffic circus with a central fountain at the northern tip of the lake. Why is it called Silk Street? Because it was once full of silk merchants — though nowadays its shops sell Russian and Japanese watches, French perfumes and cosmetics, imported fashions, Chinese and Vietnamese ceramics and even camouflaged sun-caps inscribed with the words "United States Army." Around Silk Street there are other streets still more commonly known by the products they sell — and these range from rice to auto parts.

The Old Quarter is the symbol of the new entrepreneurial spirit that's gripped northern Vietnam after four decades of Marxist control. Virtually every inch of the

area has a shop or pavement vendor operating on it. To the north, the huge **Dong Xuan Market** has several floors packed with electronic goods, household products, linenwear and merchandise of every description. An open market for vegetables and wet goods sprawls around it — crowded beyond imagination every morning with rural vendors in their conical raffia-covered hats, hauling bicycles and bamboo baskets full of produce. On the northern side of this melee, you'll find a small **Taoist temple**, surrounded by gardens but hidden discreetly behind high walls, with prayer halls adorned with images of Taoist gods, Buddhas and immortals.

At the northeastern end of the Old Quarter, the dramatic 1,682-m **Long Bien Bridge**,

bombed and strafed repeatedly during the Vietnam War until American POWs were put to work repairing it, provides another key conduit into the district. Every morning the bridge throngs with farmers and workers from the countryside beyond the Red River, many of them struggling across with bicycles and baskets loaded with chickens, ducks, vegetables and fruit to grab a vantage point in the turmoil around Dong Xuan.

The Old Quarter is Hanoi's most exciting and evocative adventure — getting right among the common people. As such, it reflects the city's main attraction and its drawbacks. For all its historical and cultural

ABOVE: Hanoi's Central Market lies roughly at the borderline of the city's old and "new" quarters.

monuments, Hanoi is at its most interesting when you're simply out in the streets. It offers something perhaps more pronounced here than in any other city in Indo-China except Phnom Penh — a previously restricted, disciplined, austere society suddenly bursting into business, and enjoying every minute of it.

WHERE TO STAY

When it comes to five-star accommodation and service, there's really only one game in

town — the 250-room **Pullman Metropole** on Ngo Quyen Street, (☎ (4) 266919). Formerly the Thong Ngat Hotel, it was elegantly renovated by the French group Accor to capture the fledgling but growing business travel market in Hanoi. The result is a deluxe property incorporating all its former colonial architecture and fittings, with a top-class bar and main Continental restaurant, business center, swimming pool and plans for more rooms, executive offices and conference facilities and additional restaurants. Rates are naturally high — in the US$114 to US$194 range for a double room.

Outside the Metropole, there's a crop of much older, mostly undeveloped hotels and guesthouses that may not have the same high-class facilities but are far more reminiscent of pre-socialist Indo-China. The **Bac Nam**, two blocks south of the Metropole on Ngo Quyen Street, has undergone a renovation of sorts — new air-conditioning, TV and refrigerators in each room and that sort of thing. But while it offers clean and comfortable budget accommodation at around

US$30 to US$60 a night, its ground floor lobby opens Indo-China-style out on to the street, where you can sit in tiny bamboo chairs in the buzzing heat of an evening and watch the city pedal by. It also has an excellent Vietnamese/Chinese restaurant and an open dining room on the roof.

The old **Dan Chu Hotel** at 29 Trang Tien Street (☎ (4) 253323) and the towering **Hoa Bien Hotel** (☎ (4) 253315) at the corner of Ngo Quyen and Ly Thuong Kiet streets are rustic establishments still living an era of dusty red velvet and beaded curtains. But both have dining rooms which, while quite basic and gloomy, offer some of the best budget meals in town, with Vietnamese and Western menus; and the Hoa Bien has a rooftop bar which catches the evening breeze in the hot, torpid summer months. Their rates are similarly in the US$30 to US$60 range for high-ceilinged double rooms with air-conditioning, fans and mosquito nets.

There are two other interesting establishments in this category if you're looking for something with a difference. The **Guest House** (that's what it's called) at 33C Pham Ngu Lao Street (☎ (4) 252896) has clean, comfortable accommodation and particularly friendly staff, and has become a mecca for visiting photographers and correspondents. The nearby **Guest House of the Ministry of Defence** (Nha Khach Bo Quoc Phong) at 33A Pham Ngu Lao (☎ (4) 265539) is "excellent but a little more expensive," according to a colleague who stayed there in late 1992.

If you want to move up into the US$50 to US$70 a night range, and don't mind being nearly four kilometers out of the city center, the **Thang Loi Hotel** on Yen Phu Street (☎ (4) 258211) has the attraction of being right on the shore of West Lake. It also has resort-style bungalow accommodation, a swimming pool and tennis courts.

It bears mentioning that these are obviously proven properties that offer comfort and good service and do not fall into the cheap backpacker category of hotels. As in most major cities of Indo-China, tourism development is moving so fast that they may well have been renovated, upgraded and elevated to a higher rate category by the time you go there. New hotels, mainly in the four- and five-star category, will almost certainly have been opened, too; so you'd be well advised to get an updated list from your travel agent before making your trip.

WHERE TO EAT

The Pullman Metropole's **Continental** restaurant offers the most elegant setting and best cuisine in Hanoi, and the highest prices: dinner for four with drinks can set you back about US$150. My favorite restaurant is the **Piano Bar**, which is actually a three-storey eating place in a converted private home at 50 Hang Vai Street (((4) 232423) in the Old Quarter. Its Vietnamese and Chinese food are excellently prepared, and it specializes in one particularly succulent dish, stuffed crab in the shell. The staff are young, friendly and helpful, and on most nights you'll be entertained by a pianist and cellist playing Chopin, Bach, Mozart and other Western classics. The **Restaurant Bistrot** at 34 Tran Hung Dao (((4) 266136) is another highly recommended but fairly expensive establishment, largely because its chef used to work at the French embassy in Hanoi.

As already mentioned, if you're looking for a varied, good-quality menu offering Vietnamese, Chinese and Western dishes at less than US$10 for two people, the **Hoa Bien**, **Dan Chu** and **Bac Nam** hotel restaurants won't disappoint you. They also serve breakfast and lunch. Then there's a series of small family restaurants which have become famous for the focus they put on good food at the expense of the setting and decor — places like **Cha Ca Restaurant** at 14 Cha Ca Street just north of Hoan Kiem Lake, which has become renowned for its fried fish dishes; **Restaurant 22** at 22 Hang Can Street; **Restaurant 202** at 202 Pho Hue, south of Hoan Kiem Lake; and the **Chau Thanh Restaurant** at 60 Ngo Phat Loc Street in the Old Quarter.

Again, restaurant prices are constantly on the rise in Hanoi as these establishments become more and more popular. New restaurants are opening up literally every month to cater for the growing influx of business travelers and tourists. The restaurants listed here are the pioneers of a swiftly developing city for which any guidebook will just as quickly be outdated.

Vietnam: the North

HOW TO GET AROUND

Although all the major hotels have cars, mini-buses and limousines at their disposal, there is really only one way to get around Hanoi — by pedal-cyclo. These open contraptions, something akin to a front-end loader powered by a bicycle, are perfect for a city in which the people, the noise, the smells and the passing kaleidoscope of tree-fringed shop-houses, markets and villas lose their impact and exoticism

from behind the darkened glass of an air-conditioned car or van. The cyclo drivers are mostly ex-war veterans, most of them educated and polite, and they'll take you anywhere you want to go. The cost: about US$1 per hour, and the idea is to select a driver you particularly like and hire him on an exclusive stand-by basis at US$10 a day. Some of the cyclos have seats wide enough to take two people, which makes cyclo-touring in Hanoi especially enjoyable for couples.

OPPOSITE: The Pullman Metropole hotel has prepared Hanoi for a new era of international commerce. ABOVE: Cyclo drivers still provide city's main transportation.

At the time of writing, some of the hotels were able to arrange for guests to rent bicycles, and this may now be more widespread. It's also likely that visitors can rent motorcycles now, and the best place to check this out is at your hotel front desk or among a cluster of bicycle and motorbike shops near Restaurant 202 on Pho Hue Street.

SPECIAL SIGHTS

Lenin Park on Dien Bien Phu Street, next to the quite stylish Chinese Embassy, now has

one of the very few statues of Lenin left in the communist world. The Hanoi state circus often performs here, too.

Souvenir portraits of Ho Chi Minh, painted in heroic revolutionary style, can be found on the **Thong Nhat Book Store** at the corner of Ngo Quyen and Trang Tien Streets, just south of the Pullman Metropole.

Across the intersection, still on Trang Tien Street, you'll find one of Hanoi's **official ice cream outlets**. In the evenings, the pavement and street are literally packed with people of all ages, along with their bicycles and motorbikes, relishing a treat which is taken for granted anywhere else in the world.

The **Palace**, which is a small stadium-shaped concrete building on Pho Nha Trung Street west of Hoan Kiem Lake is a dance hall — one of several now flourishing around Hanoi — which features nightly pop concerts by the city's growing legion of Western-style rock bands. It's an interesting nightspot to visit for a number of reasons — it's a chance to chat with Hanoi's new trend-setting younger generation, experience the talent the Vietnamese have for modern rock music and witness another aspect of the nation's current transition, with tangos and

fox-trots interspersed with the heavy metal numbers.

The state-owned **Bank for Foreign Trade**, a huge domed mausoleum of a building at 47 Le Thai To Street, just north of the Pullman Metropole, is worth popping into not just to change money and travelers checks but also to take a look at the consequences of inflation in Vietnam. Behind the tellers' wickets and just about anywhere there's floor space available, you'll see vast stacks of Vietnamese banknotes, all of them counted and packaged, ready for the day's foreign exchange transactions. On a filming trip there in 1992, I exchanged US$1,900 into *dong*. I walked out almost staggering under a pile of notes totaling 20-million *dong*.

HAIPHONG

This rather dilapidated coastal city, 103 km (64 miles) east of Hanoi, is strategically important as the key port of northern Vietnam. You may recall it was a prime United States bombing target during the Vietnam War, but the regular presence of Soviet freighters — and the risk of a much more dangerous conflict — saved it from destruction. Nonetheless, it was mined by the Americans to halt the flow of Soviet military supplies.

bags on long cords, rhythmically scooping the water from one plot to another.

Because of the speed with which the day heats up, the farmers and their families are usually working in the fields at first light and are on their way home to shelter and rest by mid-morning. In the late afternoon, the road becomes a social spot for families gathering to chat and enjoy the cooling air. Along the route you'll see towns and villages set far back from the road, some of them sporting church spires. If you're traveling individually, it's possible to arrange with your

Although it has a few cultural spots of its own to show off, Haiphong's main attraction is the trip it takes to get there — the main road from Hanoi passing through some of the prettiest and most idyllic ricelands of the Red River Delta. It's along this route that you'll see Vietnam's still-traditional farming methods in action — fat water buffaloes ploughing the flooded paddies; women in conical hats sowing seed and fertilizer by hand; flocks of ducks being shepherded to new feeding grounds; rows of bamboo hats nodding and bending amid the green and golden rice as the womenfolk harvest it with small curved knives; and, here and there, girls irrigating the paddies with a simple but most ingenious system of leather water-

driver to make a detour here and there. If you're with a group, forget it: like much of Asia, the average Vietnamese driver or tour guide has one responsibility in mind — to get you as fast as possible to wherever you're supposed to go.

Haiphong also provides the main access to Halong Bay, north Vietnam's dramatic holiday "resort," and the route north to this beautiful bay is even prettier than the approach from Hanoi — taking two river ferries and running through farming hamlets before

OPPOSITE: LEFT Hanoi market vendor and RIGHT ramshackle public transport. Street barber ABOVE bears scars of the Vietnam War. OVERLEAF: Fantastic karst outcrops, island caves and grottoes promise a rich tourism future for North Vietnam's Ha Long Bay.

melting into an almost surrealistic landscape of green fields and towering karst formations.

WHAT TO SEE

Haiphong is a bustling commercial city, a market-place, and much of its character comes from being an international entrepìt. Its shops and open markets offer consumer goods straight off the ships that you may not find in Hanoi, along with second-hand products — anything from motorcycles to rice-cookers — brought in by enterprising crews from around Asia. Unless you're looking for trade or investment opportunities, you'll probably not stay there for any length of time. But if you're on an overnight stop to or from Halong Bay there are a couple of places you might want to visit.

Du Hang Pagoda

Located to the south of the city center on Chua Du Hang Street, this 300-year-old pagoda is architecturally interesting but has been rebuilt several times.

Hang Kenh

This district to the southwest of the downtown area is noted for two cultural attractions — a **communal house** on Hang Kenh Street featuring a collection of 500 wooden sculptures, and the 65-year-old **Hang Kenh Tapestry Factory** which produces traditional and modern woolen carpets and tapestries for export.

Do Son Beach

This hilly coastal peninsula and beach, 21 km (13 miles) southeast of Haiphong, has slumbered since the colonial days when it was a popular seaside resort for the French. But in early 1993 it was about to become Haiphong's prime attraction in the competition for tourism. According to newspaper reports, some 100 investors from Hong Kong, Taiwan and China had established a joint venture to develop a US$300 million casino as part of a hotel and recreation center at Do Son. Work on the casino was scheduled for completion at the end of the year, and up to 200 "experts and croupiers" were to be brought in from Hong Kong and Macau to train the Vietnamese staff. The gaming palace would be open only to

foreigners, the reports said, and was expected to have a turnover of US$3 million a day.

Cat Ba Island

For a far more tranquil stopover in the Haiphong region, it may now be possible to travel freely — without a special permit, that is — to the virtually undiscovered island of Cat Ba, 30 km (19 miles) east of the port city. In 1986, much of Cat Ba was proclaimed a national park to protect its natural beauty — jungles, freshwater lakes, dramatic karst hills with waterfalls and subterranean caves — and a series of offshore reefs rich in coral and marine life. The island is a natural wilderness, except for the southern coastal areas around the town of Cat Hai where a population of around 12,000 busies itself with fishing, forestry and the growing of rice and fruit. There's a daily ferry from Haiphong to Cat Hai, and it's worth checking with Haiphong Tourism at 15 Le Dai Hanh Street (℃ (31) 47486) on whether Cat Ba is now open to foreign tourism.

WHERE TO STAY

Being an international port, there are a number of hotels in Haiphong, but most of them are sadly run-down. The best establishment in town, the **Hotel du Commerce** at 62 Dien Bien Phu Street (℃ (31) 42706), is a place of faded French elegance operated by Haiphong Tourism which offered three-bed suites at US$40 a night when I was there. However, like most state-run properties in Vietnam its restaurant was disappointing and so was its service.

The **Hong Bang Hotel** at 64 Dien Bien Phu Street (℃ (31) 42229), offers clean rooms with twin beds, TV and laundry service at US$35 a night, while the **Huong Sen Hotel** at 16 Minh Khai Street (℃ (31) 42992) is more in the budget range — US$12 to US$20 a night twin-share and, according to a photographer friend who stayed there, "girls available at the bar!"

WHERE TO EAT

There are a number of small, friendly restaurants and coffee shops which have sprung up around the central market area of Haiphong, most of them offering very palatable Vietnamese food. But according to

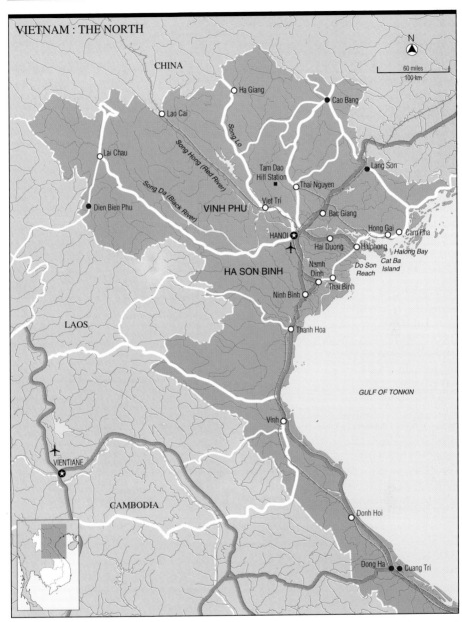

VIETNAM : THE NORTH

my photographer friend, the **Bong Sen Restaurant** at 15 Nguyen Duc Canh Street (℃ (31) 46019) is "the best Western and Vietnamese restaurant in Haiphong City."

HALONG BAY

Halong Bay, 60 km (37 miles) north of Haiphong, is a place where you step right back in time — its waters dotted with the tattered bat-wing sails of old sailing junks that have virtually disappeared from China's coastal seas. When you place these beautiful working antiques against the dramatic backdrop of some 3,000 chalk and limestone formations that form a dragon's tail across the bay, it doesn't take much to imagine what Halong Bay will be some time in the future — one of Vietnam's prime tourist resorts.

Vietnam: the North

At the moment, Halong Bay is rustic and undeveloped, a holiday spot for workers and cadres from Hanoi and Haiphong, but not much more than that. Its beachfront hotels are run-down and overpriced in terms of their standard of accommodation and service, and its tourist services are limited to a couple of old launches which can be hired for day-trips to the closest karst formations. Some of the "islands" themselves have huge caves and grottoes in them — some of them extending up to two kilometers into the rock — but whether you'll really be able to enjoy the stalactites and other formations within them depends on the efficiency of your guides: they're generally helpful and enthusiastic, but their smoky kerosene lamps don't really throw much light around you.

For all that, Halong Bay is a physical attraction certainly worth seeing, and to be seen now before the developers get their hands on it. It won't be long before its shores are crowded with modern resort hotels, its waters full of windsurfers, sailing vessels and jet-skis and its karst islets surrounded by scuba dive-boats.

WHERE TO STAY

The towns of **Bay Chai** and **Hong Gai** are the tourist centers of Halong Bay, facing each other across a narrow harbor linked by an old vehicular ferry. Bay Chai, set on a long pebbled beach, is where the hotels are. Most of them charge about the same rate for foreigners — US$25 to US$45 depending on the floor you're on and whether you want air-conditioning or ceiling fans. Rooms are clean, and most have open balconies with a sea view, but the bathrooms are often antique and there are the usual breakdowns and other problems with the electricity that you find right across Indo-China. They all have friendly and quite helpful managers who'll arrange sightseeing tours and excursions through the karst islands. The **Phuong Dong Hotel** (℃ (31) 46323) is recommended for its service, and was charging US$22 to US$25 a night for comfortable double rooms when I was there. Other establishments like the **Ha Long** (℃ (31) 46238), **Bach Long** (℃ (31) 46281) and **Hoang Long** (℃ (31) 46264) ranged from US$25 to US$45, though you could bargain

your way down to US$30 a night on a weekday. One point to keep in mind is that these hotels offer the only quality **restaurants** in Halong Bay, although new seafood restaurants are being built around the town's market, reflecting the new wealth that's going into this previously impoverished region.

GETTING THERE

There's only one way to get to Halong Bay, by road from Haiphong. The journey can take up to three hours, allowing for photo stops, but it's really the most satisfying way to approach the resort — there are picturesque inland ports fringed by karst hills amid the rural setting along the way. In 1993, the only way to arrange transport was through a three-day tour, including hotel accommodation, organized by Vietnam Tourism in Hanoi, but local officials were talking about a plan to modernize the road and to launch a daily helicopter service from Haiphong or Hanoi as the first step in developing Halong Bay's resort potential.

SPECIAL SIGHTS

Just after dawn along Bai Chai beach, the Halong Bay **fishing fleet** sells part of its catch to market vendors — mostly women — who paddle out to their junks in small, oval-shaped, woven-bamboo "coracles" that are the feature of this region. An early morning ferry crossing to **Hong Gai** brings you to Halong Bay's key fishing port where the junks are based, and another bustling fish and seafood market.

Beyond Hong Gai, you can drive around a series of quite dramatic headlands and through farming valleys to **Cam Pha**, a small coal-mining town. Cam Pha is significant because it's one of the key areas from which the refugees fled to Hong Kong and other parts of Southeast Asia to escape poverty during the early years of austerity after the war. Now, Cam Pha is a regional center of European Community aid aimed at providing a basic infrastructure for new industries, and the town features a vocational training school where local teen-agers and returning refugees are taught tailoring and dressmaking, simple electronic engineering, woodwork and furniture-making and a craft that offers a big immediate potential in Vietnam, motorcycle mechanics. There's another larger European Community training school in Haiphong.

AROUND THE NORTH

As already mentioned, travel beyond the Hanoi–Haiphong–Halong Bay route has been restricted through poor roads, a lack of transportation and an understandable re-

of *arhats* dating from the eighteenth century. At Thay Pagoda, there are sculptures of another 18 *arhats* and a stage in the middle of a small lake where one of Vietnam's unique performing arts—**water puppets**—is staged for pilgrims and visitors at the temple's annual festival in the third lunar month (March/April).

HUONG TICH MOUNTAIN

This karst hillside, whose name translates into "Mountain of the Fragrant Traces," lies

luctance by the government to expose particularly isolated, undeveloped societies to foreigners too quickly. However, with reports that travel permits may be lifted generally in Vietnam, it may now be possible to get off the beaten track to some of the following locations:

TAY PHUONG

This small village about 40 km (25 miles) southwest of Hanoi features two interesting Buddhist temples, the **Tay Phuong Pagoda** and nearby **Thay Pagoda**. At Tay Phuong, the complex is actually three small pagodas arranged in the shape of a water buffalo and they contain more than 70 wooden carvings

60 km (37 miles) southwest of Hanoi in Ha Son Binh province and has a Buddhist temple complex, **Chua Hong** (The Perfume Pagoda), built into it.

TAM DAO HILL STATION

Built by the French in 1907, this hilltop town is north Vietnam's version of the south's Da Lat — a highland retreat where the colonials sought relief in the hottest summer months. Some of their villas are still there, though suffering considerably from years of neglect, but the environment has

ABOVE: Fishing family in Ha Long Bay — this region spawned much of the refugee migration to Hong Kong.

Vietnam: the North

remained fairly pristine — a series of wooded peaks offering hitchhiking amid giant ferns and wild orchids, and visits to hilltribe hamlets. Tam Dao is in Vinh Phu province about 85 km (53 miles) northwest of Hanoi.

CUC PHUONG NATIONAL PARK

This large nature reserve, established in 1962, is a hilly rain-forest embracing a wide variety of flora, insects, animals and reptiles. But it's a long way from Hanoi —140 km

(87 miles) by road, with a lot of potholes and washed-out sections along the way. However, the park has a guesthouse at its headquarters for overnight visits.

HOA LU

This ancient capital of northern Vietnam, which flourished in the Dinh and Early Le dynasties between 968 and 1009, lies in a region of karst hills two hours south of Hanoi on Route 1, not far from Ninh Binh. Though once rivaling Hue as a royal citadel, all that's

ABOVE: Hanoi street vendor. OPPOSITE: Municipal Theatre in Haiphong TOP. Decrepit vehicular ferries BOTTOM provide the only means of crossing Haiphong's Cam River.

now left are two temples commemorating the emperors of that time — one of them featuring early weaponry, among other relics — and a shrine to Confucius.

LANG SON

This riverside border town, 150 km (93 miles) north of Hanoi, was the last stop in Vietnam on the railway to Nanning, China, when the link was operating. It sprang back into prominence in the 1979 border war, when it was almost destroyed by invading Chinese forces. In the reconciliation that's followed, Lang Son has become one of the major conduits of trade — official and unofficial — between the two former enemies, and will no doubt profit from its strategic position in the future. It's also likely that the railway will be rebuilt, just as there are plans to reopen the equally strategic rail link between Hanoi and Kunming in Yunnan province.

DIEN BIEN PHU

For all its notoriety, there's really no reason to try to get to this sprawling battle site, just 16 km (10 miles) from the border with Laos and 420 km (260 miles) northwest of Hanoi, unless you're a former Legionnaire or scholar of the first Indo-China War. Although there's a museum on the spot where the French capitulated, overrun by thousands of Viet Minh troops, the hills around it recall virtually nothing of the labyrinth of communist trenches and bunkers from which they launched their human wave assaults. Likewise, there's nothing left that's reminiscent in any way of the tremendous struggle and heroism of the Vietnamese battle-plan — heavy artillery and antiaircraft guns hauled through dense jungles and up steep hillsides, often under constant bombing attacks, to lay siege to the French positions. Dien Bien Phu is perhaps a place in which to contemplate man's follies, just as Khe Sanh, the site of the 1967 entrapment of the United States Marines, is in the south. Other than that, the two-day drive from Hanoi is perhaps the only other real reason to go there — a scenic tour of mountain vistas, tea plantations and wide plateaux matched only by the journey from Saigon to Dalat.

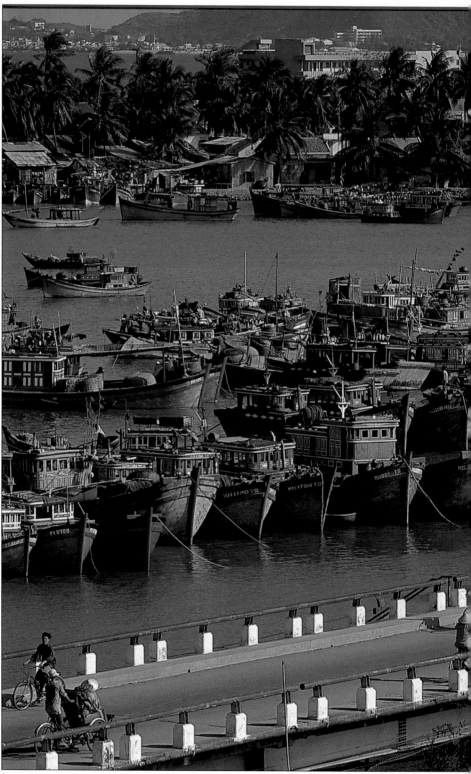

Vietnam:
the South

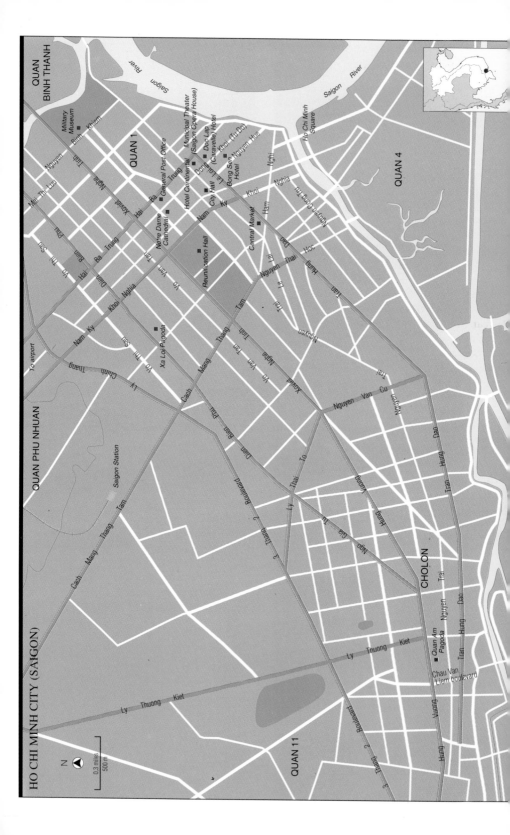

HO CHI MINH CITY (SAIGON)

N

0.3 miles
500 m

QUAN PHU NHUAN

QUAN BINH THANH

QUAN 1

QUAN 4

QUAN 11

CHOLON

Saigon River

Saigon River

To airport

Ho Chi Minh Square

Military Museum

Municipal Theater (Saigon Opera House)

Doc Lap (Caravelle) Hotel

Bong Sen Hotel

Hotel Continental

General Post Office

Notre Dame Cathedral

City Hall

Central Market

Reunification Hall

Xa Loi Pagoda

Saigon Station

Quan Am Pagoda

Chau Van Liem boulevard

Ly Thuong Kiet

Ly Thuong Kiet

Cach Mang Thang Tam

Cach Mang Thang Tam

Nguyen Thi Minh Khai

Mai Thi Luu

Dien Bien Phu

Ba Trung

Hai Ba Trung

Xo Viet

Nam Ky Khoi Nghia

Vo Thi Sau

Ly Chinh Thang

Dien Bien Phu

Nguyen Trai

Tran Hung Dao

Nguyen Van Cu

Vo Van Tan

Nguyen Dinh Chieu

Tran Hung Dao

Nguyen Thi Minh Khai

Le Loi

Nguyen Hue

Khoi Thu Do

Nguyen Hue

Dong Khoi

Nam Ky

Ham Nghi

Nguyen Cong Tru

Hung Vuong

Nguyen Chi Thanh

Ly Thai To

Nguyen Trai

Tran Hung Dao

Hung

Boulevard 2 Thang 3

Binh Khiem

Nguyen

SAIGON (HO CHI MINH CITY)

When the unique Saigon Floating Hotel was hauled up from Australia's Great Barrier Reef and positioned in the Saigon River in 1989, its Australian management company prudently suggested it be named the Floating Hotel of Ho Chi Minh City. No, said the municipal authorities, pointing out that while no-one outside Asia would really have a clue where Ho Chi Minh City was, just about everyone has heard of Saigon.

The issue reflected a number of nuances in Saigon's relationship with the party leadership in Hanoi, not the least of them being its special status in the "new" Vietnam — the fact that, in the struggle to rebuild the economy, it's been there before. In the war years, fattened with billions of American dollars, the city was regarded as one of the richest, most advanced and certainly one of the most sophisticated in Asia. It came under heavy suppression after the fall of 1975, many of its intellectuals and entrepreneurs — the ones that didn't make it to freedom in the United States, that is — jailed or put into re-education camps, and a system of high-security paranoia imposed on the population generally. Now, of course, Saigon's former capitalists are back in favor, vital to the campaign to pull the economy up by its bootstraps; but the authorities here are still somewhat stricter than those in Hanoi — fearing this industrious, freewheeling city, with its large Chinese population, will get out of hand. The north-south divide is still a potentially damaging specter in reunited Vietnam.

As a visitor, it's difficult to sense this underlying tension in Saigon today, the city fattening again on foreign investment, its downtown streets and markets packed with imported luxuries and the latest Japanese, Korean and Taiwanese consumer appliances, its traffic jams already rivaling those of Bangkok and its people engaged in an absolute frenzy of free enterprise. Saigon is rapidly regaining its wartime status as the capitalist center of Indo-China, while at the same time clinging grimly to the landmarks of its past — rapid economic and social development taking place in a metropolis that, by modern standards, is still confined, almost village-like, and quaintly antique.

Although its sprawling suburbs are beginning to boom with new housing and joint-venture factories, the inner city is still principally two main districts — a downtown business area which extends southeast from the elegant Notre Dame Cathedral to the Saigon River, centered on Dong Khoi Street (known as Tu Do Street during the war), and its teeming Chinatown, Cholon, to the west. Dong Khoi Street, still called Tu Do on some current city maps, and two

parallel streets, Nguyen Hue and Hai Ba Trung, are where most of the key commercial centers, travel agencies, airline offices, banks, cultural centers and hotels are located. The Central Market (Ben Thanh), lying west of Dong Khoi on Le Loi Boulevard, fronts a wide traffic circus from which the main access streets to Cholon radiate.

When I say that Saigon is still quaintly antique, I mean that the downtown area that most visitors today will be familiar with, is very much what it was in the war — an everyday itinerary that takes in Notre Dame Cathedral and the adjacent Post Office, an architectural masterpiece in its own right,

Elegant City Hall and Ho Chi Minh Square in central Saigon.

and extends south down Dong Khoi to the stately Hotel Continental and Municipal Theater, west past the Eden Center and public square to the Rex Hotel and on to the Central Market, then south again via the Doc Lap (Caravelle) Hotel on Dong Khoi or a series of mid-street photo and souvenir kiosks on Nguyen Hue to the Saigon River waterfront. I'm certainly not saying that this is all there is to the city, but within this relatively confined grid of streets, there's virtually everything that any visitor would need to either re-create the Saigon of 1968 or

tree-shaded public park sprawls to its rear. Closed by the communists after the 1975 takeover of Saigon, Notre Dame is now flourishing again, with services beginning at dawn each day.

General Post Office
Lying alongside Notre Dame, the GPO is another striking architectural landmark, built in 1886, which somehow combines an opulence of colonial bas-relief and charming shuttered windows with a vast central hall reminiscent of a canopied Victorian railway

capture the essence of this southern capital in its latest lusty renaissance.

WHAT TO SEE

Notre Dame Cathedral
If we take a closer look at this downtown itinerary first, Notre Dame is the starting point — an elegant blend of red brick and white stone with two soaring spired towers that faces directly down Dong Khoi toward the Saigon River. Built in 1877, Notre Dame and its spires, viewed across a green cloudbank of trees, add an almost pastoral touch to Saigon's skyline. The cathedral fronts a sweeping square which features a tall white statue of the Virgin Mary, and a well-kept

station. Veterans of the war years will remember it for its postage stamps — they had no glue on them, and you had to hunt around for a paste pot to stick them on the envelopes. Today, it's still the main communications center for the Saigonese, but the hotels have now usurped it as a provider of telephone, fax and postal services for visitors.

Eden Center
This huge weather-stained, balconied French commercial block, south on Dong Khoi and right opposite the Hotel Continental, was best-known during the Vietnam War for its

ABOVE: Saigon's Opera House (Municipal Theatre) flanked by the famed Hotel Continental in downtown Saigon. OPPOSITE: Notre Dame Cathedral, Saigon.

"Bank of India" — a thriving black-market currency exchange operated by Indian merchants who are reported to have been executed during one of President Nguyen Van Thieu's patently selective crackdowns on corruption. It's still a rabbit-warren of company offices, souvenir shops, tailors and other enterprises, along with Vietnam Airlines and Cathay Pacific Airways reservations centers and the Queen Bee dancing club; and one of its most famous old establishments is back in business — the Givral Patisserie and Cafe, right on the corner of Dong Khoi and Le Loi Boulevard, which veterans will remember for its afternoon coffee and ice cream.

Hotel Continental

This stately old *grande dame* of Saigon, renowned for evening drinks and the shoeshine boys in its open verandah bar during the war, is as much a cultural attraction as a hotel. Somehow, it's managed to tart itself up yet come down a peg or two — the famous verandah bar now closed in and turned into a high-priced Italian restaurant, the standard of service lowered since it became a state-run establishment. Still, it's something of a treat to breakfast on hot croissants, baguettes and coffee in its inner garden courtyard, once favored by foreign correspondents, and the old girl will no doubt attract a new suitor one day — an international hotel management group capable of putting some dash, charm and sophistication back into her.

Municipal Theater

Right across from the Continental and facing Le Loi Boulevard, the Saigon Opera House, as it's more commonly known, with its high arched entrance, was the South Vietnam's National Assembly during the war. Now it's the city's main cultural center, with concerts, recitals, plays and performances by Saigon's new crop of pop artists staged there every night. The pop singers tour the city's main clubs each evening, performing a couple of numbers at each venue before racing on to the next. At the Opera House, they're allowed two songs, and if the audience applauds loudly enough they're invited to give an encore.

During the war, the gardened square opposite this building featured a huge, grotesque concrete sculpture depicting a United States soldier and his ARVN (Army of the Republic of Vietnam) comrade charging into battle. But cynicism was so rife among correspondents and United States troops that it was regarded as a United States soldier pushing his Vietnamese counterpart into the fight. Even more cynical was another popular unofficial description — a United States soldier and ARVN comrade attacking the National Assembly.

Rex Hotel

This renovated hotel on Le Loi Boulevard, right across Ho Chi Minh Square from the Eden Center, also deserves special mention for its wartime role. This was the Rex BOQ (Bachelor Officer's Quarters for United States

personnel) during the war, heavily sand-bagged against Viet Cong attack and one of the focal points of the United States and international media. Its ground floor, occu-pied by JUSPAO (Joint United States Public Affairs Office), was where the famous "Five O'Clock Follies" — a daily media briefing on the war — was staged. The establishment's rooftop was a sprawling officer's bar and mess with a stage for regular go- go dance shows, and a viewpoint from which visitors could watch the war at night — the tracers from jet cannon and helicopter machine-guns pouring into the city's outer suburbs.

Today, the Rex's rooftop features a bi-zarre exhibition of glass-fiber Disney-style elephants, deer and other decorations. It's open bar is still a good position from which

to view the city's skyline. Other than that, state control of the hotel and its new reputa-tion as a business travelers' venue has given its management a somewhat arrogant atti-tude toward guests and visitors.

City Hall
Facing Ho Chi Minh Square and a bronze statue of "Uncle Ho" embracing a child, this excellent restoration of one of Saigon's pret-tiest colonial buildings was once the Hôtel de Ville and is now the headquarters of the People's Committee. Its opulently decorated facade and clock tower provide a backdrop to the square, which is crowded weekends with Vietnamese sightseers and families

ABOVE: Saigon's Municipal Theatre was the often stormy legistlature of South Vietnam during the war.

taking snapshots. Those who know this location from the old days will be interested to learn that the Rex Cinema is still there, and is still virtually packed out most evenings.

Central Market (Ben Thanh)

This huge hangar-like covered market, west on Le Loi Boulevard from the Rex Hotel, has to be seen to be believed — the words "crowded" and "bustling" just do not do justice to this incredible bazaar. Shoppers come here in their hordes to pick and jostle their way through stalls packed cheek-to-

jowl and piled high with consumer and household goods, shoes, cheap clothing, poultry, fish and just about every other product and provision you can name. The market has entrances on all four sides, so you can get in quite easily. Getting out is another thing altogether, such is the general crush of shoppers, wandering hawkers, beggars, monks and novices cadging alms, and kids selling lottery tickets. Another teeming open market fills the streets around Ben Thanh, and around that there are shops and boutiques selling home electronics, watches, jewelry, luggage and fashion clothing. What you won't

ABOVE and OPPOSITE: Saigon street life — as in most cities in Indo-China, two wheels often do the work of four.

find much of these days is the United States war-surplus material — helmets, fatigues, webbing, canteens, combat watches, tents and hammocks, C-rations and other goods — which filled Ben Thanh during the war.

Ham Nghi Market

Some United States military supplies, along with souvenir Zippo lighters, can still be found in the newer market area which has mushroomed in Ham Nghi Street, leading northwest from the Saigon River to Ben Thanh. Ham Nghi itself has become one of

Saigon's main venues for consumer electronics, its shops and sidewalks piled with Japanese and Taiwanese TVs, VCRs, hi-fis and computer equipment. In the streets between Ham Nghi and Nguyen Hue, a sprawling open market is also full of imported watches, video games and other electronic products.

Brodard's Restaurant

I highlight this particular establishment, located on Dong Khoi Street a block south of the Doc Lap (Caravelle) Hotel, because of its staying power. Brodard's was a popular cafe during the war, the place to go for traditional *café filtre* — Vietnamese coffee filtered on to a thick bed of sweetened condensed milk —

and crisp French bread filled with paté, cheese and ham. The restaurant was run-down even then, a kind of faded Art Deco joint with aging waiters who intimidated Anglo-Saxon customers with their impeccable French. I'm rather glad to say it hasn't changed, though there's every chance that it might have been renovated by now. Aside from the food and the correct but good-natured waiters, Brodard's has a wide picture window fronting Dong Khoi where it's been a tradition for years to sit and watch the passing parade of activity on one of the city's key thoroughfares.

stations where you can get a cold beer, the latest Western pop and a girl to sit and stroke your hand, pull the hairs on your wrists, slap and pinch you playfully a few times and then inquire "Which hotel you stay?"

Apocalypse Now
Dong Du Street, which runs west from Dong Khoi from just outside the Bong Sen Hotel, is notable for three attractions — the **Saigon Business Center**, set up to provide modern office facilities and communications for incoming joint-venture companies; the

Hai Ba Trung
As you continue south toward the river, the lower end of Hai Ba Trung Street, running parallel to Dong Khoi, is one place where Saigon's bars have reopened with a vengeance. They're pretty basic places — formica-topped tables, a touch of colored lighting, a thumping hi-fi system and a team of young and not-so-young bar girls — but as a nostalgia trip all that's really missing are the off-duty GIs and menacing military police. In the new tradition of nightlife in Saigon, these bars and others like them all over the city — especially in the streets east of Notre Dame Cathedral and on the long boulevards toward Cholon — are labeled cafes or cafeterias. But their role is the same—little comfort

Central Saigon Mosque, thrusts its white minarets up through the general concrete decor of this district; and a series of **new tourist bars** centered on the Apocalypse Now. As the name suggests, Apocalypse Now is a rather trendy attempt to capitalize on war nostalgia — it blasts the sound-track from Robin Williams' *Good Morning Vietnam* at least once a night—and it attracts the trendiest of backpackers and local expatriates. Still, it's a good place to blow your mind for an evening, cross-check travel information and contemplate the problem it's going to be to get back to your hotel — large crowds of beggars, hawkers and cyclo drivers tend to rush you the moment you step out to go home. Another bar called **Good Morning**

Vietnam had opened up opposite Apocalypse Now when I was there, and there may well be several others in Dong Du by now.

Me Linh (Hero) Square

All main streets in this central downtown area eventually converge on a vast piazza at the Saigon River, where a towering statue of the hero himself, Tran Hung Dao, who led the resistance against the invading Mongols in 1287, challenges the striking six-deck blue-and-white facade of the Saigon Floating Hotel. Me Linh Square is interesting

ing girls" and the grand old Majestic Hotel with its famous Cyclo Bar, look over the Siren Floating Restaurant, a gaggle of tourist cruise boats and a large cruise junk operated by a French entrepreneur. To the west, the waterfront is dominated by the city's naval headquarters and a huge dry-dock which spends most of its time repairing battered Russian freighters. Hero Square is where you can hire a launch to tour the Port of Saigon, cruising among the container ships and something that's now quite unique to south Vietnam — high-prowed lighters and

because it's extended Saigon's tourist district south to the river, and if you view it from its best vantage point, the top deck of the Floating Hotel, you'll sense how important this sprawling circus will become in the future. On its northern boundary, the new Shakes Pub and Restaurant looms over old hostess bars and the southern ends of Nguyen Hue, Dong Khoi and Hai Ba Trung Streets. To the east along the waterfront, the neon-lit Riverside Hotel, a clean and friendly place with a good restaurant, the Seaman's Club, which advertises an "ideal dancing room with charming, dainty danc-

cargo junks with big eyes painted on their bows.

War Museum

Actually called the **War Crimes Museum**, this complex of old buildings at the intersection of Le Qui Don and Vo Van Tan streets is an emotionally debilitating exhibition of American and allied atrocities committed during the Vietnam War. The My Lai massacre, the Phoenix Program torture sessions, the Viet Cong suspects being hurled from helicopters — it's all there, presented in room after room of photographic displays. It says nothing, obviously, about communist atrocities, and it seems a shame that this litany of crime and suffering could not have

ABOVE: Downed US jet in the Revolutionary Museum, Saigon. OPPOSITE: City's Ho Chi Minh Memorial rests alongside the Saigon River port.

embraced the mutual savagery and collapse of human value that distinguished the Vietnam War from other contemporary conflicts. What particularly struck me amid this harrowing scene was the frame and rotors of a helicopter gunship nestled under a tree in front of the museum, a huge Long Tom artillery piece — which once hurled shells across the Demilitarized Zone into North Vietnam — nearby, and, alongside that, one of the guillotines that the French imported to deal with nationalist activists. Other than that, it was fascinating to view news pictures

see the number of war veterans, cripples and amputees that these revolutionary governments tossed into the streets after the victory to fend for themselves. However, this museum is located right next to the new Rex Tennis Restaurant and Bar at the corner of Ly Tu Trong and Nam Ky Khoi Nghia streets, north of the Rex Hotel, where you can play a game of tennis in the afternoon and then sit outside with a drink and snack in the museum grounds and contemplate Russian antiaircraft guns and a captured American tank and helicopter which were

of the political giants of the Vietnam War — Lyndon B. Johnson, Dean Rusk, Robert McNamara, Ambassador Elsworth Bunker, Gen William Westmoreland, Presidents Nguyen Cao Ky and Nguyen Van Thieu — and to contemplate how ignominiously they've passed into history since.

Museum of the Revolution
Located in what was once Gia Long Palace, built in 1886, this is a typical Indo-Chinese shrine to the communist triumph, with all the politically correct, pro-Soviet paraphernalia that you'll find in similar museums in Vientiane and Phnom Penh. To be honest with you, I find them deathly boring and obviously propagandist especially when I

used in the 1975 liberation. You'll find the same sort of equipment on show at the Military Museum on Nguyen Binh Khiem Street near the Saigon Zoo.

History Museum
Also located on Nguyen Binh Khiem Street, at the zoo entrance, this museum traces Vietnamese history from the Bronze Age to the post-1975 era, and includes a research library. Prior to the fall of Saigon it was the National Museum of South Vietnam, built in 1929 by the Société des Études Indochinoises.

United States Embassy
After the panic and confusion of 1975, when this huge square edifice was one of the key

evacuation points in Saigon, it was simply left empty to rot by the revolutionary government. Thus, its high wall, barbed wire and gunposts are still there, and so too are its fluted anti-rocket facade and festoons of telecommunications aerials on its roof. In 1992, an oil company had leased part of the complex, but the main chancellery was still a crumbling, dripping empty shell. Of course, with the embargo close to being lifted, the Americans may well be back there now, but the word at that time was that they would set up a new embassy in the MIA Office in Hanoi.

Reunification Hall

This contemporary building, erected in 1966 in a blend of Western and Asian design, lies in sweeping grounds surrounded by a decorative steel fence beyond the public park to the west of Notre Dame Cathedral. It's a significant landmark — it was the Presidential Palace, and home of Nguyen Van Thieu, from the height of the Vietnam War until Thieu was finally forced from office shortly before the fall of 1975. It's also significant as a symbol of the communist triumph — you may recall the TV news scenes of the tank crashing through the palace's main gates, and the Viet Cong soldier rushing to fly the revolutionary flag from its balcony. Nowadays, Reunification Hall is a tourist attraction, open all days except Sunday, and a trade exhibition center. Ex-President Nguyen Cao Ky, once famous for his dashing flight-suits, pearl-handled revolvers and equally flamboyant First Lady, now runs a

store in Los Angeles. As for Thieu, he died a virtually forgotten recluse in England.

Ho Ky Hoa Park

Ho Ky Hoa Park lies north of 3 Thang 2 Boulevard, one of the major roads running west through the Cholon area. It has an amusement park with fairground rides for children and a small boating lake. What makes it an attraction of sorts, however, is an old restaurant alongside the lake where newly-weds congregate after the ceremony to have their pictures taken. It's a chance to relax with the Saigonese and witness some of the color and tradition that's returning to their lives.

Orchid Farm

More than 1,000 varieties of orchid, including two named after Richard Nixon and Joseph Stalin, are grown at this farm, located 15 km (nine miles) from downtown Saigon along the highway to the former United States military base at Bien Hoa. Visits can be arranged through your hotel desk or travel agency, and the best time to go there is in January or February when the plants are in full bloom.

The Temple Tour

There are a great many Buddhist and Taoist temples in Saigon and Cholon, some of them neglected and dilapidated, others gleaming with renovation work for the tourist market. The oldest is the **Giac Lam Pagoda**, northwest of Cholon at 118 Lac Long Quan Street, which was built in 1744 but completely restored in 1900. This temple, and the nearby **Giac Vien Pagoda** at 247 Lac Long Quan Street, dating back to the late eighteenth century, feature a great many relics and images including white statues of the Goddess of Mercy.

Xa Loi Pagoda, at 89 Ba Huyen Thanh Quan Street, north of Ben Thanh Market, is probably more significant because it was here that dissident monks burned themselves to death in protest against the Diem regime in the early 1960s. The ritual suicides followed a raid by government forces in 1963 in which the temple's 400 monks and nuns were arrested. Another quite historical place is the **Tran Hung Dao Temple** at

ABOVE: Scarred and dilapidated former United States Embassy in Saigon. OPPOSITE: Street vendors outside Saigon's Mariammam Hindu Temple.

36 Vo Thi Sau Street, dedicated to the hero of Vietnam's battle to defeat the invading Mongols of China's Yuan dynasty. Two much newer temples are the **Dai Giac Pagoda** at 112 Nguyen Van Troi Street on the way to the airport, and the **Vinh Nghiem Pagoda**, built in 1971 with the support of the Japan-Vietnam Friendship Society, whose eight-storey pagoda towers over the suburban sprawl of Nam Ky Khoi Nghia Street.

Among the Chinese temples of Saigon and Cholon, the **Emperor of Jade Pagoda** at 73 Mai Thi Luu Street is the biggest and most opulent. Dedicated to both the Buddhist and Taoist creeds, it was built in 1909 by Saigon's Cantonese community, and its courtyards and three main prayer halls are crowded with images of the divinities, including the Goddess of Mercy, the Sakyamuni Buddha and the Emperor of Jade himself. The city's Fujianese immigrants built their main shrine, **Phung Son Tu Pagoda**, at 338 Nguyen Cong Tru Street, and it's dedicated not only to the Goddess of Mercy but the Guardian Spirit of Happiness and Virtue as well.

In Cholon, the renowned **Quan Am Pagoda** at 12 Lao Tu Street is generally recognized as the district's most important shrine, but you'll find a far more picturesque temple, the **Thien Hau Pagoda**, dedicated to the Goddess of the Sea, in crowded Nguyen Trai Street. Above the entrance to this small but colorfully restored temple there's an elaborate ceramic frieze featuring mandarins, immortals and scenes from the Taoist legends. The main hall is reminiscent of the famous Man Mo Temple in Hong Kong — huge coils of smoking incense hanging from its rafters. Not far from this temple on Nguyen Trai Street, another Chinese place of worship, the **Nghia An Hoi Quan Pagoda**, features gilded bas-relief wood carvings and images of Thien Hau and the Guardian Spirit of Happiness and Virtue.

Saigon Racecourse
This old racetrack and its bare, concrete, time-worn grandstand have sprung back to life since a Hong Kong investor revived the weekly races in 1991. But don't expect anything as grand as Kentucky or Ascot: the horses look underfed, the jockeys are pre-teen boys and the race goers are usually the

city's poorer people — laborers and cyclo drivers. However, it's another place where you can watch the Vietnamese, and Cholon Chinese, at play, and if you decide on a flutter of your own the bets are generally just a few hundred *dong*. Races are held every Saturday afternoon, and the track is located north of Cholon near Ho Ky Hoa Park.

Cholon
During the communist Tet Offensive of 1968, the Viet Cong infiltrated Saigon through this urban beehive, populated by ethnic

Chinese, to the west of the downtown area. And when you see its densely crowded streets you'll appreciate why. Cholon isn't just a hum of activity, it's more like a pandemonium, and you'll find you're exhausted after a couple of hours battling its traffic and pedestrians. Chinese immigrants began setting up shop here in 1778 and, as in most expatriate Chinese communities in Asia, they've suffered their share of discrimination in times of nationalist fervor. During the Vietnam War, many were regarded as profiteers, and they came under a certain amount of repression after 1975. Many of them fled Vietnam, making up a large percentage of the boat people who made it to Hong Kong. However, their value to Vietnam's economic revival has put them back in favor today: it's estimated that for every dollar in foreign investment that comes into Vietnam, two dollars is brought in unofficially by the people of Cholon through family contacts in Hong Kong, Taiwan and other Asian countries.

Hung Vuong and Chau Van Liem boulevards are the central thoroughfares of Cholon, and the district's most crowded spots are the recently renovated Binh Tay Market and nearby long-distance bus station. The district has a number of hotels, headed in terms of comfort and service by

US$230 for a room with a balcony; the new Century Hotel on Nguyen Hue Street (((8) 293168) offers standard and superior double rooms at US$160 and US$200; the Caravelle (Doc Lap) Hotel (((8) 293704) has first class and deluxe double rooms at US$81.40 and US$129.80; the Rex Hotel (((8) 292185) charges US$71.50 for a superior double room and US$82.50 for the deluxe version, though you could get a comfortable single room for US$59.40; the Mondial Hotel (((8) 296291) costs US$50 for standard double occupancy, rising to US$70 and US$80 for

the Arc En Ciel at 52-56 Tan Da Street (((8) 252550), and a great many Chinese restaurants; but you'd be advised to stay in central Saigon and treat the tumult of Cholon as a day-trip by pedal-cyclo.

WHERE TO STAY

Saigon has a lot of hotels, but if you want international-class service (and I would certainly advise against going too far down-market) the upper category is the one you should confine yourselves to. Taking it from the top, the Hotel Continental, (((8) 299201) double rooms in the US$88 to US$115 range; the Saigon Floating Hotel (((8) 290783) charging US$195 for a standard room and

superior and deluxe; rates at the Bong Sen Hotel (((8) 291516) ranged from US$44 for a second class double room to US$72 for a junior suite, with a first class double priced at US$50 in its adjacent, cheaper annex; and on the riverfront, the elegant Hotel Majestic, although in need of an interior renovation, has clean double rooms priced from US$47 to US$80.

One notch below this category, the Palace Hotel (((8) 292404) s charges US$55 for a regular double room, US$63 for a first class double and US$72 for a "corner room"; the Huong Sen Hotel (((8) 291415), managed

OPPOSITE: Entrance to Thien Hau Temple in Cholon. ABOVE: Worshipper at main altar of the Jade Pagoda.

by the Bong Sen, has doubles at US$30 to US$55; the **Riverside Hotel** (**(** (8) 224038), across Hero Square from the Saigon Floating Hotel, has rooms in the US$35 to US$50 range; and, at the bottom end of the comfort category, the **Saigon Hotel** on Dong Du Street (**(** (8) 299734) offers first class doubles at US$36.

These rates are obviously quite high for a city that's hardly back in the tourist mainstream — caused by shortage of first-class properties and a big influx of business travelers. The shortage may well have been

eased by now — the Hong Kong-based New World International group had started work on a new five-star property near Ben Thanh Market in 1993. But whatever, the hotels listed above guarantee cleanliness, a telephone in the room and at least reasonably good restaurants. To go below that range may well mean much cheaper accommodation, but be advised that a lot of the real budget hotels in Saigon and Cholon have not only poor service and food but prostitutes who are likely to hammer on your door at all hours of the night.

WHERE TO EAT

While all the hotels that I've recommended offer excellent Vietnamese, Chinese and Continental restaurants, one remarkable thing about Saigon is the speed with which its

ABOVE: The Saigon Floating Hotel, shipped to the Saigon River from Australia's Great Barrier Reef. OPPOSITE (TOP): Rex Hotel roof garden, formerly a United States officer's mess. BOTTOME: Rex Hotel reception area.

restaurant industry has recovered elsewhere. I've already mentioned **Brodard's**, the **Rex Tennis Restaurant** and the **Givral Patisserie and Cafe** as traditional or unusual one-off places for a drink and snack, but they're only a mild taste of what Saigon has in store.

The ornate, neon-lit **Maxim's** (**(** (8) 296676) near the Majestic Hotel is flourishing again with an extensive Continental and Chinese menu, live pop music and disco dancing. But, as in the war years, it's at the top-end of Saigon's nightlife, and it's expensive. For excellent Vietnamese cuisine at more reasonable prices, the **Thanh Nien Restaurant** is a friendly, open-air establishment in the grounds of what used to be the hub of colonial society in Saigon, the Cercle Sportif. You'll find the Thanh Nien at 11 Nguyen Van Chiem (**(** (8) 225909) and, having eaten there several times, I thoroughly recommend it. **Vietnam House** (**(** (8) 291623) on Dong Khoi Street, just down from the Bong Sen Hotel, is an opulently renovated establishment with a ground-floor bar and upstairs restaurant, traditionally costumed staff, a very sophisticated Vietnamese menu and prices to match. **Le Mekong** (**(** (8) 292277), a French restaurant which, like the Piano Bar in Hanoi, has taken over several floors of a private residence, has very good cuisine but will set you back US$80 to US$100 for a meal for four with drinks. You'll find this restaurant at 159 Ky Con Street west of Ben Thanh Market. If your tastes run to surf'n'turf, the **City Bar and Grill** at 63 Dong Khoi Street (**(** (8) 298006) is popular with Western expatriates in Saigon.

For Vietnamese cuisine and seafood, the **Siren Floating Restaurant** (**(** (8) 225402) on the riverfront near the Saigon Floating Hotel is worth trying, while **The River Cafe Restaurant** (**(** (8) 293734) at 5–7 Ho Huan Nghiep, in a backstreet off Hero Square, has been recommended by one diner as "very clean and civilized with excellent food." Other well-known Vietnamese restaurants are **Nha Hang Cay Dua** (**(** (8) 298467) at 54 Le Lai Street, **Tri Kyh Restaurant** (**(** (8) 240968) at 82 Tran Huy Lieu Street and **Phu Nhuan Restaurant** (**(** (8) 240183) at 8 Truong Quoc Dung Street opposite the Dai Giac Pagoda.

Western-style pubs and taverns are also sprouting up to cater for business expatriates,

and aside from **Shakes Pub and Restaurant** on Hero Square opposite the Saigon Floating Hotel, the most popular establishment is the **Tiger Tavern** (℡ (8) 222738) which is uptown at 227 Dong Khoi Street, close to Notre Dame Cathedral.

Two other well-known establishments bear special mention. The **Queen Bee** restaurant and dancing club (℡ (8) 292589) in the Eden Center is a place where you can not only dine in style on Vietnamese or Continental cuisine but also enjoy one of the best discos in town—a full menu of Western and

Vietnamese pop, heavy metal and everything from the quick-step to tango, with excellent lighting effects, that goes on to two in the morning. Then there's **La Bibliotheque**, a most elegant and evocative French/Vietnamese restaurant which Mme Nguyen Phuoc Dai, a former lawyer and member of the war-time National Assembly, operates in her villa at 84A Nguyen Du Street, close to Notre Dame Cathedral. The dining room itself is set in what was once Mme Dai's library, so you eat surrounded by shelves packed with old law books.

Contrast of color and commerce — fleeting boats CENTER on Vung Tau beach flanked by Saigon's Hotel Continental LEFT and OPPOSITE Vung Tau's Seabreeze Hotel.

TRANSPORT

Again, although the hotels and travel agencies in Saigon have limos, cars and minivans available, the pedal-cyclo is really the only way to get around the city. When I was there, they were charging the equivalent of US$0.5 a short trip, but I would advise you strike a deal at US$1 per hour, and unlimited mileage. It's best to hire one around your hotel, and let the concierge know which one it is. Like Hanoi, most of the drivers are war

veterans, and most are helpful and polite — but you occasionally run into one who'll hassle you for extra money while you're on the road. You'll find a rank of small white Renault taxis on Le Loi opposite the Rex Hotel. They're quaint, but I recommend you avoid using them. They're the same vehicles that operated during the war, and probably the same drivers, and they were notorious for breakdowns and fierce arguments over the fare at the end of the journey.

SPECIAL SIGHTS

Each Saturday and Sunday evening, stand in the broad square between the Hotel Continental and Municipal Theater and watch thousands of adults and teen-agers ride their motorbikes down Dong Khoi Street to the riverfront. It's quite a spectacle, a continuous stream of headlights and roaring engines that flows until after midnight; and there's an interesting story to it. According to some reports, this is a social outing that began as a weekly demonstration, a show of force, by the Saigonese to remind the city's communist authorities and the government in Hanoi that this is a city not to be messed about with.

Have a late afternoon beer or *citron pressé* on the roof of the Rex Hotel. Try to ignore

the awful decorations, but enjoy the panorama that this downtown eyrie provides. Have another drink on the top deck of the Saigon Floating Hotel and view another sweeping perspective of Saigon — the vast circus of Hero Square on one side, the container ships, ferries and fat-bellied rice-barges plying the Saigon River on the other.

Just north of the Hotel Continental on Dong Khoi, there's an open-air bar where you can sit out on the lawn in the heat of the night, listen to a surprisingly pleasant repertoire of pop music and watch the city go by. It's a place where you can relax, recover from the city's daytime bedlam and capture an impression or two of what Saigon must have been in more stately times.

VUNG TAU

Once a popular seaside resort under its French name, Cap Saint Jacques, Vung Tau is now a special economic zone and a center of the oil exploration industry in south Vietnam. As such, the huge pylons and steel decks of offshore oil rigs rear over the port area as you enter the town and, with some of the world's leading oil multinationals now working leases in the South China Sea, it's obvious that Vung Tau is going to be

noted more for industry than recreation in the future.

The beaches here are not that good, but Vung Tau makes up for this with a thriving fishing port, a couple of good Buddhist temples and some fine seafood restaurants. Other than that, it's a relaxing day-trip out of Saigon, and the 128 km (79 miles) drive takes you through farmland and a number of bustling rural villages.

WHAT TO SEE

A wander right around the Vung Tau peninsula, from **Front Beach** to **Back Beach**, takes in just about everything of any note, including the old Russian Compound where Soviet oil workers were housed until most of their Vietsovpetro leases were transferred to Western companies after the collapse of the Cold War. The fishing fleet moors at Front Beach, which is fringed with tall palms, but I wouldn't recommend taking a swim there. Aside from a huge statue of Jesus Christ, erected as late as 1974 at the southern tip of the peninsula, Vung Tau's prime attraction is the **Niet Ban Tinh Xa temple**, on the waterfront between Front Beach and the statue, which features a fairly spectacular reclining Buddha and a huge bronze bell on its roof. In short, Vung

lishment, the **Canadian Hotel** (℃ (64) 9852), has standard and superior rooms at US$48 and US$68, a business center and tennis court. It's located at 48 Quang Trung Street. There are dozens of other hotels and guesthouses in Vung Tau, but most cater for Vietnamese holiday-makers from Saigon and have pretty basic facilities.

WHERE TO EAT

The most highly recommended restaurant in town is the **Hue Anh** at 446 Truong Cong

Tau is a welcome break from Saigon, a place for relaxation and people-watching but nothing much more to write home about.

WHERE TO STAY

The **SHC (Seabreeze) Hotel** (℃ (64) 2392) is the best in town, under foreign management with rooms at around US$40 a night. You'll find it at 11 Nguyen Trai Street. The **Grand Hotel** (℃ (64) 2306) at 26 Quang Trung Street is cheaper — between US$10 and US$25 a night, depending on the room — and is operated by OSCAT, a joint-venture which services the oil industry. Another estab-

Dinh Street (℃ (64) 9563) which specializes in Chinese food and seafood. Another good seafood restaurant is the **Huong Bien** at 47 Quang Trung Street on Front Beach. At Back Beach, the **Thang Muoi** (℃ (64) 2515) at 7–9 Thuy Van Street, is the biggest and best.

CON DAU ISLANDS

This group of 14 islands 180 km (112 miles) south of Vung Tau is just beginning to create interest as a possible resort location after years of notoriety as a penal colony. The main island, **Con Son**, was used as a prison for political dissidents by the French and the United States-backed Saigon government

Fishing boats and boatyards on the river at Rach Gia in the Mekong Delta.

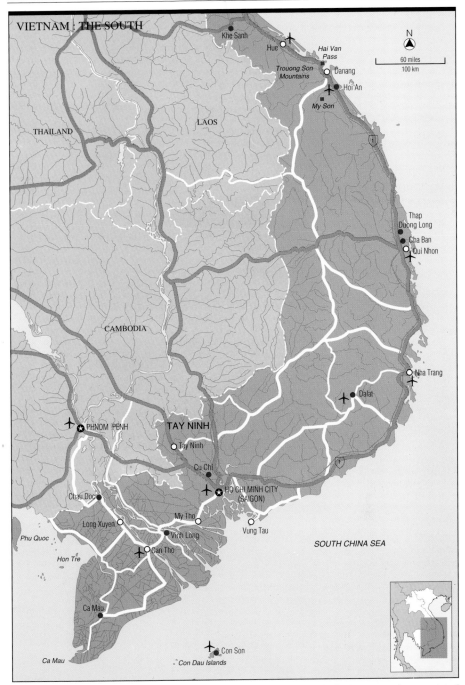

VIETNAM : THE SOUTH

during the war, and the inhuman conditions in which they were incarcerated are illustrated in its Revolutionary Museum. However, Con Son has good beaches, coral reefs, teak and pine forests and a farming community raising tropical fruits, and it's linked with Vung Tau by a helicopter service operated by Vietnam Airlines. It's highly likely that you'll hear a lot more about this island as the tourism developers move in, and it would be worth while checking whether it now has facilities for foreigners.

CU CHI

The famous tunnels of Cu Chi, the vast **underground network** from which the Viet Cong fought in the Vietnam War, have now taken their place among the great wonders of military lore. They're also one of the prime tourist attractions outside Saigon. But before you go rushing there, be advised that you'll see very little of the more than 200-km labyrinth of tunnels, staging camps, hospitals, operations bunkers and whatever that defied American bombing, defoliation and constant search-and-destroy missions throughout the war. What you'll see is a couple of bunkers and tunnels that have been widened to accommodate bulky Westerners, and Japanese and Taiwanese tourists firing AK-47 assault rifles on a nearby range. In other words, forget it: you'd learn a lot more simply by reading the book *The Tunnels of Cu Chi* by Tom Mangold and John Penycate (Random House, New York, 1985). If you do go there — and you'll need to book a half-day or one-day tour through your hotel or travel agency in Saigon — there's something far more significant than the "show" tunnels to see: a nearby military cemetery contains the graves of some 8,000 Viet Cong soldiers who died defending the network.

THE DELTA TOWNS

The Vietnamese call the **Mekong River** *Song Cuu Long* — River of the Nine Dragons — and its vast delta, culminating a 4,500 km (2,800 mile) journey from the Tibetan plateau, is the nation's richest agricultural area. After flowing down through Laos and Cambodia, the river divides into two main arms at Phnom Penh. As they reach the delta, the upper arm flows into the South China Sea at Vinh Long and the lower at Can Tho. In the rainy season from May to October, the entire delta region is virtually a lake, the river's various arms and tributaries flooding the rice fields as far as the eye can see. In the dry season it's a dazzling sheet of green or gold, depending on the progress of the crop, punctuated by tiny hamlets hidden in copses of tall palms. For all its power and

fame, however, the Mekong River is surprisingly lifeless when you compare it with the great rivers of Europe. Wherever you are, in Laos, Cambodia or the delta region, there's very little river traffic — just an occasional ferry or fishing boat. But it's the towns along its banks, and their busy markets, which bring this vast waterway alive — and nowhere is this more evident than in the Mekong Delta.

There are a great many interesting delta towns, but whether you'll be able to get to them depends on the state of transportation.

In the Vietnam War, the helicopter and C-130 transport, or armed river patrol craft, were the only means of reaching most of its key centers. By early 1993 it was possible to go by road or take public ferries (with the right permit) from Saigon to My Tho, Can Tho and Vinh Long, but getting deep into the delta beyond there may well be a challenge even now.

MY THO

This is the closest delta town to Saigon — just 70 km (43 miles) away — and the trip

OPPOSITE: Young worshippers in the Tay An Pagoda at Chau Doc. ABOVE: The cathedral at My Tho in the Mekong Delta.

itself is perhaps more interesting than the destination. Right from the edge of Saigon's suburbs, you pass through rural areas so pretty that it's like driving through a well-kept garden — the rice fields dotted with hamlets and white stone ancestral tombs. Alternatively, a ferry leaves Saigon at 11 am each day, departing from a dock at the end of Ham Nghi Boulevard, and takes six hours to reach Mytho. Once there, there's not much to see except the **central market**, the 100-year-old **Catholic church** and the **Mekong riverfront**. The **temple of the Coconut** delta, 104 km (65 miles) south of My Tho. Again, it provides a delightful day-trip through the delta farm lands, via two river ferry crossings; and again, although it has a distinctive Khmer Buddhist **temple**, the **Munirangsyaram Pagoda**, its central market is the key attraction.

LONG XUYEN

Located upriver to the north of Can Tho, this provincial capital is remarkable for its religious texture. Up until the stirrings of the

Monk, located on a small island in the river, is touted as a local attraction, but quite frankly it's not worth the ferry ride — unless you simply want to be able to say you traveled on the mighty Mekong River. Mytho is another day-trip, an enjoyable excursion out of Saigon to the edge of one of the world's greatest food bowls.

CAN THO

It takes up to five hours by car to reach Can Tho City, the administrative capital of the

Vietnam War, it was the center of an armed religious sect called the Hoa Hao, which rejects churches or temples and the priesthood. Obviously, it has left nothing really to show for itself. The city's main showplace, in fact, is its huge **Catholic church**, completed in 1973 and accommodating 1,000 worshipers. In event of an overnight stay, the **Long Xuyen Hotel** is regarded as the city's best, with air-conditioned rooms for US$20 to US$25 a night and a top-floor dance hall, but the service is quite awful.

CHAU DOC

Lying not far from the Cambodian border, this small town is notable as the main access point

PREVIOUS PAGE: The magnificent Munirangsyaram Pagoda at My Tho. ABOVE: Fishing boats at rest in Rach Gia. OPPOSITE: Flamboyant midday mass at the bizarre Cao Dai Temple in Tay Ninh.

116   Vietnam: the South

to **Tan Chau**, a famous **silk-weaving district**, and **Sam Mountain**, a Buddhist center with many temples and grottoes around its slopes. The **Tay An Pagoda** is one of the finest, featuring hundreds of carved wooden images, but there's a more interesting one, the **Cavern Pagoda**, halfway up the mountain, with images of Sakyamuni Buddha and the Goddess of Mercy. The **Chau Doc Hotel** is recommended as the best in town, with clean rooms at US$20 to US$25 a night. But the food isn't that good, and the staff speak very little English.

DELTA ISLANDS

Beyond the delta towns, the islands of **Phu Quoc** and **Ca Mau** are worth keeping an eye on for tourism development — improved access, that is, and decent hotels. Of the two Phu Quoc has the most potential — a mountainous, forested island in the Gulf of Thailand 15 km (nine miles) south of the Cambodian border which is said to have excellent unspoilt beaches and coral diving spots. The island is served by a weekly Vietnam Airlines flight from Saigon, but it'll probably be some time before it comes on stream as a regular travel destination.

TAY NINH

Notwithstanding the beauty of the delta region, it's to the north of Saigon that you must go to find south Vietnam's most fascinating cultural attractions. And Tay Ninh, located three hours by road to the northwest, right on the Cambodian border, is the center of one of its unique cultural spectacles, the **Cao Dai**.

The Cao Dai is a religious sect (see page 59) founded in 1926 which embraces

all religions — mixing Christianity, Buddhism, Islam, Confucianism and even Taoism into its creed and featuring a priesthood and structure based on the Roman Catholic Church. Its most revered symbol is the "divine eye," which may or may not have been borrowed from Middle Eastern Islam and is found on all Cao Dai temples in Tay Ninh province and the Mekong Delta. The eye is the focal point of the sect's spectacular **Great Temple at Long Hoa**, four kilometers from Tay Ninh City, where extravagantly costumed services are held four times a day, beginning at 6 am, and tourists are beginning to rival the congregations in numbers.

But whether it's becoming a tourist attraction or not, a Cao Dai service is something to behold — massed ranks of cardinals, priests and white-robed male and female clergy parading into the vast, pillared, opulently decorated hall of the Great Temple to pray before the altar and divine eye to the chanting of choirs and rattle and chop of wooden instruments. The Cao Dai lay women are friendly, dignified and only too willing to explain the principles and rituals of Cao Daism to you before the services begin.

Tay Ninh itself is otherwise more interesting for its location and contemporary history than anything else. With Cambodian

major resort development. And no wonder. Nha Trang has a six-kilometer main beach that rivals Pattaya in Thailand, dozens of reportedly pristine diving and snorkeling locations among its 71 islands and a cultural backdrop that features relics of the ancient Cham kingdom of central Vietnam.

The city and its gently curving beach lie 448 km (278 miles) from Saigon on a promontory that runs south of the Cai River estuary. A beachfront road, Tran Phu Boulevard, extends south from the river, becoming Tu Do Street as it approaches the peninsula.

territory bordering it on three sides, the city was a key United States Special Forces base monitoring the southern end of the Ho Chi Minh Trail during the war. It also came under the pressure of Khmer Rouge border attacks before Vietnam invaded its neighbor in 1979.

Tay Ninh is another day-trip from Saigon, very easy to reach along a highway which passes through delightful rural scenery — and a spiritual experience you'll never forget.

The business and administrative district, including the Nha Trang Hotel, are to the north of the airport, close to the estuary.

Three islands lie reasonably close offshore. **Bamboo Island** (Hon Tre) is the closest and biggest, reached easily by boat, and has an adjacent island, **Hon Mun** (Ebony Island) which is already becoming noted for its snorkeling spots. **Salangane** (Hon Yen), which is 17 km (11 miles) out at sea, is one of several islands famous for their annual harvest of swift's nests which are the essential ingredient of bird's nest soup.

NHA TRANG

Like Halong Bay in the north, this beautiful coastal city and its islands are earmarked for

OPPOSITE LEFT and RIGHT: Cao Dai prayer hall in Long Hoa. ABOVE: Fishing nets laid out for repairs at Hai Duang near Nha Trang.

WHAT TO SEE

Cham Towers

Only four of the original eight Cham towers of Po Nagar (The Lady of the City) are now standing, but they are among the finest examples of Cham architecture in central Vietnam. The towers were built between the seventh and twelfth centuries, but the site — two kilometers north of Nha Trang on the opposite bank of the Cai River — was a Hindu place of worship as early as the second century. Among these surviving monuments, the North Tower is the oldest but best preserved, featuring stone wall carvings of Shiva dancing to the accompaniment of musicians, a stone gong and drum and, in the lofty main chamber, a 10-armed stone image of the goddess Uma. There's a small museum close to this site exhibiting other Cham relics. The three other towers are less illustrious, but two of them have stone lingas in their main chambers and the other, the Northeast Tower, features more bas-relief sculptures. The North Tower was built in 817 after the original temple complex had been destroyed by Indonesian raiders.

Long Son Pagoda

This far more contemporary relic, built in the late nineteenth century, lies in the shadow of a towering white Buddha seated on a lotus west of the city center on 23 Thang 10 Street. The temple's most distinctive feature is mosaic dragons which adorn its entrance and roofs.

Nha Trang Cathedral

Located on Thai Nguyen Street, which is the eastern extension of 23 Thang 10 Street, this Gothic structure with its stained glass windows looks medieval but is even more contemporary — completed in 1933.

Oceanographic Institute

Just about every example of marine and birdlife in Nha Trang's waters has been brought to this aquarium and exhibition hall — the sea creatures displayed in ground-floor tanks and the birds stuffed and put on show in the hall behind. The institute is six kilometers south of Nha Trang City at Cau

Da, right on the tip of the peninsula. As with most museums and cultural exhibits in Indo-China, it's tacky and everything's stuck behind thick glass, and to get a much more realistic picture of the region's environmental charms you'd be better off going snorkeling or visiting Mieu Island, four kilometers off the promontory, where you can visit a fish and seafood breeding farm and enjoy a drink in a cafe set on stilts over the water.

Bao Dai's Villas

Bao Dai was the last emperor of Vietnam who attempted to form an anti-communist state still linked with France during the first Indo-China War, then abdicated when the Viet Minh achieved victory. His five seaside

villas, built in the 1920s, are just north of the Oceanographic Institute and testify to the lifestyle which he obviously feared was threatened by the nationalist forces. President Nguyen Van Thieu took advantage of them when he was in power, and after the 1975 victory they became dachas for the communist hierarchy. They're now tourist guesthouses, renovated and air-conditioned, with lush gardens and excellent views of Nha Trang and the nearby islands.

WHERE TO STAY

Bao Dai's Villas (℃ (58) 22449) provide the most dramatic accommodation in Nha Trang — one of those surviving colonial-style com-plexes where you can get a feel for the grander days of Indo-China. At last report, they were offering huge double rooms at US$35 a night, but you can expect to be paying somewhere in the US$50 to US$70 range now. You'll find them close to the tip of the peninsula, with oil storage tanks located behind them. In the city center, the seven-storey **Nha Trang Hotel** at 133 Thong Nhat Street (℃ (58) 22347) is a cut above everything else, while on Nha Trang Beach you'll find that the **Thang Loi Hotel** (℃ (58) 22241), **Thong Nhat Hotel** (℃ (58) 22966) and **Hai Yen Hotel** (℃ (58) 22828) are the closest you'll get to international-class comfort and service.

Morning at the fish market in Qui Nhon.

WHERE TO EAT

You'll find a lot of new cafes and restaurants specializing in seafood dishes along the beachfront. But two establishments with a tradition for fine food and service are the **Lac Canh Restaurant** at 11 Hang Ca Street near the central market, which serves grilled shrimp and lobster, and the **Binh Minh Restaurant** at 64 Hoang Van Thu Street, which has an excellent Vietnamese menu.

DIVING, SNORKELING

Recreational diving isn't an organized activity yet in Nha Trang, though there may well be professional dive shops there by the time you visit. But snorkeling doesn't require tanks and sophisticated gear, and you can either take your own masks and fins or buy them in the central market. As for transport to the islands, check with your hotel or the following: The **Ship Chandler Company**, 74 Tran Phu Boulevard (℃ (58) 21195) or **Khanh Hoa Province Tourism**, 1 Tran Hung Dao Street (℃ 22753).

GETTING THERE

Vietnam Airlines operates regular flights to Nha Trang from Saigon, Danang and Hanoi.

ABOVE: Vendor prepares fruit display in Dalat's central market. OPPOSITE: Dalat Cathedral LEFT built in 1931. RIGHT Morning on Dalat's central Xuan Huong Lake.

QUI NHON

Qui Nhon is the nearest coastal access to the northern Central Highlands and centers like **Pleiku** and **Kontum** where fierce battles were fought between the Americans and infiltrating North Vietnamese units during the war. Lying 238 km (148 miles) north of Nha Trang, it's also not the easiest place to get to: its airport at Phu Cat, another notorious wartime base, is 36 km (22 miles) north of the city.

Qui Nhon doesn't offer the splendid beaches and seaside charm of Nha Trang, but it's noted for its **Cham ruins**. There are three complexes: two quite spectacular towers at **Thap Doi**, close to the city center; the walled ruins of the former Cham capital, **Cha Ban**, 26 km (16 miles) to the north; and three other elaborately decorated towers, **Thap Duong Long** (Towers of Ivory) about eight kilometers beyond Cha Ban.

WHERE TO STAY

Qui Nhon hasn't yet begun developing its potential for tourism, but the **Dong Phuong Hotel** at 39 Mai Xuan Thuong Street (℃(56) 2915), the **Thanh Binh Hotel**, 17 Ly Thuong Kiet Street (℃ (56) 2041) and the beachfront **Quy Nhon Tourist Hotel**, 8 Nguyen Hue Street (℃ (56) 2401) are probably the best in town.

WHERE TO EAT

The **Tu Hai Restaurant** (℃ (56) 2582) on the upper floor of Lon Market on Phan Boi Chau Street, has an English menu and a variety of Vietnamese and seafood dishes, along with a dancing club. You might also try the **Ganh Rang Restaurant**, about three kilometers from the city center along Nguyen Hue Street, which is set on stilts in gardens right on the seafront and reportedly was frequented by the wife of Emperor Bao Dai.

DALAT

Lying 1,475 m (4,800 ft) above sea-level in the southern Central Highlands, Dalat was developed by the French as a cool, high-country retreat from the obsessive summer heat of Saigon and the Mekong Delta. They built elaborate villas there, most of them attempting to recapture the familiar architecture of Normandy and Brittany as much as provide summer relief. They also turned part of the city, now known as the French District, into a complete replica of a provincial home town, and when you stroll through it even today you'll consider they didn't do a bad job.

Much of this essentially hilly city surrounds the huge **Central Market**, with ho-

eight-hour drive, but the route is the most scenic I've encountered anywhere in Vietnam — crossing wide agricultural plains, then rising through tea and coffee plantations before climbing through densely forested hills that surround Dalat. Once there, you'll find that the city meets every description that you may have read elsewhere — it certainly does have a sense of high-country magic to it, especially in the chill of the night when, because of the altitude and clean air, the heavens are brilliant with stars — but be a bit selective about the attractions it's supposed to offer.

tels and the surviving French villas set on ridges and hillocks around it. The most spectacular hotel, the Palace, looks over Dalat's key feature, Xuan Huong Lake, which is actually a reservoir created in 1919. To the north of the lake, a sweeping low-rise hill leads to Dalat's mecca for honeymooning Vietnamese, the Valley of Love; but more about that in a moment.

ACCESS

Although there are daily Vietnam Airlines flights to Dalat from Saigon (the airport, by the way, is 30 km (19 miles) south of the city) my advice is that there's really only one way to go there — by road from Saigon. It takes an

WHAT TO SEE

Valley of Love

To explain what I mean by selective, forget the Valley of Love — it's a tawdry over-commercialized souvenir complex, popular by tradition among Vietnamese newly-weds, where the stalls are packed with stuffed wildlife of every description from the forests around Dalat. It's an environmental nightmare, and flies in the face of every effort that Vietnam is now making to preserve the wildlife that survived years of bombing and chemical defoliation during the war. The Valley of Love is also the habitat of Dalat's most absurd tourist touts — young men dressed as cowboys who offer pony rides on the half-starved beasts that they ride around town. They're good-natured enough, and can't be blamed for trying to make a buck, but unless you yearn for childhood days on the donkeys at the seaside this is one aspect of Dalat to avoid.

Other Sights

If you feel like visiting places, there are several Chinese and Vietnamese temples around the city, along with the rather striking **Dalat Cathedral**, high over the lake on

Tran Phu Street, but they're all relatively "new" places, none of them dating back further than the 1950s; and while they add a special touch to the architectural character of Dalat, you'll find much better examples elsewhere in Vietnam. The same goes for **Dalat University** and the **Domaine de Marie Couvent**. One cultural spot of particular note is **Bao Dai's Summer Palace**, a villa constructed in 1933 whose 25 rooms are full of artifacts, but even then you've got to run a gauntlet of souvenir stalls and "cowboys" and their ponies to get into the place.

But this is not to say that Dalat has little to offer. Its environment is the attraction — a place to stroll among woods, lakes and old French villas in the warm dry sunshine of day or chilly evening mists and marvel at how such a place could exist in fetid, tropical Vietnam; to drink *café filtre* and eat baguettes around the clamorous Central Market of a morning; to climb the narrow streets of the **French District**, reminiscing on that holiday so long ago in Provence. That's what Dalat's all about.

WHERE TO STAY

The five-star **Palace Hotel**, ℭ (63) 22384, at 2 Tran Phu, is now really the only place to stay in Dalat, lovingly renovated in late 1993 by a Hong Kong-based joint venture and under the management of Swiss-Belhotel, whose founder used to manage The Peninsula in Hong Kong. The 71-year-old property isn't a big hotel — not more than 43 rooms and suites — but the face-lift has remained faithful to its old French charm and fittings, and obviously it has the best restaurants and bars in Dalat. In a parallel renovation, the same company has upgraded some 17 French villas in Dalat as tourist chalets and has built Vietnam's first international-class 18-hole golf course on land north of Xuan Huong Lake. The first nine holes were opened in 1993.

Another hotel with a long tradition, **The Dalat Hotel** (ℭ (63) 2363) at 7 Tran Phu Street, close to the Palace, dates back to 1907 also underwent a major renovation in 1993. At that time it was providing "deluxe" double rooms at US$50 a night. The **Minh Tam Hotel** (ℭ (63) 2447) at 20A Khe Sanh Street, about three kilometers from the city center, is distinctive for its peaceful location amid wooded hills and its history — it was the summer villa of the infamous sister-in-law of the President Ngo Dinh Diem, Madame Nhu. Built in 1936 and renovated in 1984, its rates match those of the Dalat Hotel in town. Even more distinctive are the **Governor-General's Residence** (ℭ (63) 2093) near the intersection of Tran Hung Dao and Khoi Nghia Bac Son Streets, a late colonial building which provides suites with balconies, and **Bao Dai's Summer Palace**, where you can get a room at around US$50 a night.

Dalat is said to have about 2,500 old villas, but not many of them are in any condition to serve the tourist market. When I visited Dalat, the best way to choose one was simply to drive around, select a place that was aesthetically appealing and not run-down and ask about the tariff. The average rate was US$35 for a good clean double room or suite. If that doesn't work when you're there, ask at the Palace Hotel or the

Lam Dong Province Tourism office (℃ (63) 2125) right across the street.

WHERE TO EAT

The Palace and Dalat hotels offer the best restaurants in town, but the **Shanghai Restaurant** at 8 Khu Hoa Binh Street, close to the Central Market, has good Vietnamese, Chinese and Western food. Likewise, **La Tulipe Rouge Restaurant** (℃ (63) 2394) at 1 Nguyen Thi Minh Khai Street, also close to the market, is generally recommended. Two lake-

buses, and this is the only comfortable and convenient way to go any distance, especially to the viewpoints, waterfalls and picnic spots in the hills around the city. Otherwise, Dalat is a city made for strolling, and compact enough not to walk you off your feet.

DANANG

The approach by air to this key port of central Vietnam reveals a city surrounded by

side restaurants, the **Thuy Ta** (℃ (63) 2268), right below The Palace Hotel, and the **Thanh Thuy**, right across the lake, are well worth taking a look at.

GETTING AROUND

Small pony traps ply Dalat's downtown streets, and are an ideal way to get around the inner city. But once the poor thin-shanked beasts start to climb the hills your instinct is to jump out and give them a break. Bicycles are another ideal form of transport, but once you hit the steep hillsides you'll need to jump off and give yourself a break. Check where to rent these at your hotel desk. The major hotels provide cars and mini-

some of the most beautiful beaches, bays and hills anywhere in the country. On the flights between Hong Kong and Bangkok, which now pass right over it, you can look down on a clear day and still see the pockmarks, the bomb scrapes, of Danang's suffering during the war. As a major United States Marine base, the conduit to both the Central Highlands and base camps up toward the DMZ (Demilitarized Zone), the city was the scene of some of the fiercest fighting of the war. When it fell to the advancing communists in 1975, it became a nightmare of violence as thousands of South

OPPOSITE: Rustic "cowboys" entertain the tourists in Dalat. ABOVE: Old wooden bridge crosses the Cai River at historic Hoi An.

Vietnamese soldiers and civilian refugees fought to escape by sea to ports further south.

Revisiting Danang, my own impression was that the murder and pillage of 1975 has left its mark on the city — a bustling, enthusiastic place, anxious to achieve its potential as perhaps the most important industrial, trading and international air travel hub outside Saigon, yet psychologically damaged by that wartime incident. When I was there, Danang had an edge of nastiness about it — belligerent children and beggars crowding

around you the moment you stepped out into the streets, several incidents of major theft from hotel rooms (I had an expensive shotgun microphone stolen from mine). These were experiences I could forgive Danang for, knowing its past and having been trapped there and almost killed during one of its agonies, the Tet Offensive of 1968; and if that dark edge is still there today, I hope you can forgive it too.

Danang really has so much to look forward to. The city lies between the Han River and the South China Sea, flanked to the north and south by beautiful white-sand

ABOVE: Danang's splendid Cham Museum.
OPPOSITE: Cham ruins of Singhapura.

beaches that seem to go on forever. Untouched by development, these great swathes of beach are a resort developer's dream, ready to become Vietnam's Côte d'Azure. To its north and west, the foothills of the Central Highlands begin rising in terraced ranks over sandy bays and rice fields; and a series of coastal mountain passes lead through spectacular highlands and coastal plains toward the ancient capital, Hue.

WHAT TO SEE

Cham Museum

Located at the intersection of Tran Phu and Le Dinh Duong streets (and close to the former Danang JUSPAO Press Center, now a seafood factory), the Cham Museum is the city's prime cultural attraction. This well-planned series of open pavilions houses the world's best and most diverse exhibition of Cham relics, sandstone carvings of Shiva, Brahma and Vishnu alongside carved altars, lingas and other Hindu symbols. The artistry of most of these seventh-to fifteenth-century statues and sculptures is sensual, reflecting the essential role of fertility in this creed. Elsewhere, sculptures of apsaras, musicians and scenes from the Hindu epic Ramayana are remniscent of the temple carvings of Bali. The museum is open daily with a break from 11 am to 1 pm for lunch.

Chua Cao Dai

This Cao Dai Temple, located in Haiphong Street east of the railway station, is the biggest and most important outside Tay Ninh, serving the 20,000 or so Cao Dais who live in Danang. It was built in 1965 and, like the Great Temple of Tay Ninh, its colorful daily services are becoming a major tourist attraction.

Pagodas

There are three temples in the city area, the **Phap Lam Pagoda** in Ong Ich Khiem Street and the Tam Bao and Pho Da pagodas in Phan Chu Trinh Street. There's nothing very historical about them — the oldest was built in 1923 — but the Phap Lam Pagoda features a brass statue of Dia Tang, the God of Hell, who has most surely played a part

in Danang's recent history, and is close to the Quan Chay vegetarian restaurant.

Hai Van Pass

This 496-m (552 yards) spur in the towering barrier of the Truong Son Mountains, 30 km (19 miles) north of Danang, is the first and highest pass on the route of National Highway 1 to Hue. On both sides of the pass there's a spectacular panorama, right over Danang and its coastal headlands and bays to the south, across a valley to the first coastal plain on the way to Hue on its

Marble Mountains

There are actually five tall "mountains," all solid lumps of marble, in this Buddhist complex 11 km from Danang, each representing the five elements — fire, water, earth, wood and metal. The biggest, generally referred to as Marble Mountain itself, pitted with grottoes containing stone carvings and more recently erected stone Buddhas. Getting up and down it is a tremendous climb, even though there are steps all the way, and it's made all the more difficult by child hawkers who pester you every step

northern side. More immediately, it's interesting to watch the dilapidated long-distance "express" buses that labor to and from Saigon and Hanoi, absolutely packed to the roof with passengers and luggage, hauling themselves at a painful snail's pace up both sides of the mountain. They often break down, but everyone maintains his or her humor (or sense of resignation), waving valiantly from under trees or bushes where they shelter while the vehicle is fixed. Hai Van Pass also looks down on two of Danang's prettiest beaches, **Nam O** to the south and **Long Co** to the north — neat palm-fringed crescents of sand which will no doubt be the site of resort hotels in the years to come.

of the way trying to get you to buy joss sticks and poorly fashioned marble souvenirs. To be frank with you, Marble Mountain is hugely overrated, and unless you've got muscles of steel and lungs like blast furnaces (and a ton of patience) I'd advise you to give it a miss.

Hoi An

If you want to get a feel for the early days of Asian trading ports like Macau and Malacca, this ancient trading city 30 km (19 miles) from Danang via the Marble Mountains virtually re-creates that era. Under its original name, Faifo, it was one of the region's key entrepìts in the seventeenth and eighteenth centuries, attracting

Western as well as Asian ships. It was also the first place in Vietnam settled by Chinese and, in the 1600s, the first point of contact by Christian missionaries. Today, many of the town's homes, shophouses, warehouses, clan halls and temples remain virtually as they were in the nineteenth century, and other buildings are being restored to create a fascinating living museum. For visitors who've known Hong Kong and Macau for years, a stroll through Hoi An's narrow streets brings back vivid memories of the early Chinese commercial architecture that existed there before the development boom of the late 1960s got under way. Hoi An has a **guesthouse** at 92 Tran Phu Street, but it's really a day-trip from Danang.

My Son

This series of about 20 Cham ruins — temples, walls, gates and altars — at My Son, 60 km (37 miles) from Danang, was a key religious center of Champa from the fourth to thirteenth centuries. As such, it's probably the most important surviving relic of the Cham kingdom, and one that prevailed over centuries of damage and pillage only to become a battlefield during the Vietnam War. The Cham kings of that long heyday are thought to have been buried in what was probably a complex as sacred to the Chams as Angkor was to the Khmer Hindus and Borobudur to the Javanese Buddhists.

The ruins lie in a valley near a coffee plantation and the towering **Cat's Tooth Mountain**. While nearly 70 former structures have been identified from the stone remains around the large site, only 20 give a clue today of what this complex once looked like. These have been categorized alphabetically into 10 groups by the archaeologists, but only groups B, C and D have stood the test of time and conflict enough to satisfy the imagination. They include the eleventh century stone base and linga of a temple believed to have been first built seven centuries before; the walls of a tenth century library with bas-relief brickwork of elephants and birds; a reasonably preserved tower; and a meditation hall earmarked for renovation as a new Cham museum. Restoration

work has been going on among these sites, and the plan is to eventually restore other groups which have been reclaimed by the surrounding bushland or were badly damaged during the war. My Son is another day-trip by road from Danang.

Tra Kieu Museum

The 100-year-old Catholic church of this small town, some 20 km (12 miles) beyond My Son, is interesting enough — but it's also a museum of **Cham relics** collected from the local people by the priest. They include

ceramic artifacts bearing the features of Kala, the God of Time. Close by, another far more modern church, the Mountain Church, overlooks the stone foundations of what was once Simhapura (Lion Citadel), the first Cham capital in the fourth to eighth centuries.

WHERE TO STAY

Danang has a lot of downtown hotels, but if you can get into one along the Han River embankment you'll enjoy the view of one of Vietnam's busiest river ports. The

ABOVE: Worshippers at Marble Mountain, near Danang. OPPOSITE: Cham ruins of Singhapura.

recently built **Bach Dang Hotel** at 50 Bach Dang Street (℃ (51) 23649) is one of the most comfortable, with air-conditioned double rooms at US$42 a night and a good verandah restaurant. I wouldn't agree with the claim in its brochures that it's "elegant and delicate in service," but it does its best. Right at the northern end of the waterfront, the **Hoa Binh (Peace) Hotel** (℃ (51) 23984) next to a police post at 3 Tran Quy Cap Street, is also quite new, very friendly, charges between US$20 and US$25 a night for a double room and will throw in a TV set "at request."

Phu Street is rated one of the best in Danang for Vietnamese food, while the **Thanh Lich Restaurant** near the Bach Dang Hotel is popular with foreign businessmen. As mentioned before, the **Quan Chay Restaurant** at 484 Ong Ich Khiem Street, near the Phap Lam Pagoda, is a traditional Buddhist vegetarian establishment.

GETTING THERE

Vietnam Airlines operates daily flights to Danang from Saigon and Hanoi.

The tariff also includes breakfast. In the city center, the **Pacific Hotel** (℃ (51) 22317) on Phan Chu Trinh Street has hiked its rate for a double room up to the US$40 mark, and so has the **Orient Hotel** (℃ (51) 21266) across the street. Both these establishments are about as good as you'll get in the business district.

WHERE TO EAT

The **Bach Dang Hotel's restaurant** isn't bad — you can get a good Western breakfast with traditional coffee and a wide range of Western, Vietnamese and Chinese dishes at lunch and dinner. In the city center, the **Tu Do Restaurant** (℃ (51) 22039) at 180 Tran

HUE

A number of people who've visited Vietnam in the past couple of years have told me they didn't like Hue, largely because they expected its main attraction, the Citadel, to be far more elaborate. It once was. Although not a comparatively old city, built in 1687, Hue was the capital of southern Vietnam under the Nguyen dynasty, the last to rule Vietnam, from 1802 to 1945. During that time the Citadel, the court of the Nguyen emperors, ranked in grandeur with the Forbidden City in Beijing.

From 1945, the Citadel gradually fell into disrepair, and during the Vietnam War it was the scene of intense fighting between United States Marines and North Vietnamese regulars in the 1968 Tet Offensive. At that time more than half the population of Hue lived within its outer walls, and in the battle to drive the communists out a great deal of this national treasure was destroyed.

Like Danang, Hue suffered considerably during the war. During the Tet occupation by communist troops, some 3,000 pro-government people and Buddhist monks were executed and buried in graves all over the

south of the city limits, the tombs of the Nguyen emperors.

WHAT TO SEE

The Citadel

Although only a shadow of what it once was, the Citadel still sports its high stone ramparts and huge Ngo Mon (Meridian) Gate, the main access to the imperial enclosure. Looking at its sweeping yellow-tiled roofs, red wooden pillars and huge yellow doors, you're reminded of the Meridian

city. In 1975, Hue was one of the first major south Vietnamese cities to fall to the communists, triggering a violent mass panic in which thousands of civilians and fleeing government troops fought their way through the surrounding hills and down the coast to Danang. Now one of the south's most charming cities, it is trying to restore itself as a cultural and religious center of both north and south, and develop its textile and small manufacturing industries.

As a tourist location, Hue has a lot to offer — not just what's left of the Citadel but also the scenic Perfume River, which flows right through the city, a number of sampan communities along the inner city riverfront, one of Vietnam's most revered temples and,

Gate of the Forbidden City in Beijing, though it's not quite as majestic. Along the Citadel's outer walls, other surviving ceremonial gates, mounted with intricate carvings and other decorations, give a sense of the imperial city's former scale and authority. Sadly, the Citadel you'll visit now is really just the **Purple Forbidden City**, once the inner exclusive domain of the emperors, where the Ngo Mon Gate leads to dank lotus pools, the vast, wing-roofed **Thai Hoa (Supreme Harmony) Palace** which was used for state and

OPPOSITE: One of several idyllic, untouched beaches between Da Nang and Hue. ABOVE: The Hue Citadel is Vietnam's equivalent of China's Forbidden City. OVERLEAF: Sunrise of Hue's busy Perfume River.

ceremonial events, the **Halls of the Mandarins**, the recently renovated **Imperial Library**, featuring ornate ceramic sculptures of mandarins and other figures on its roof, and the nearby **Royal Theater**, which is now the home of the National Conservatory of Music. You're quite welcome to enter the conservatory grounds and listen to the students practicing — and catch an impromptu chamber recital if you're lucky. The **Imperial Museum**, just beyond the north wall, completes the Citadel tour — housed in another impressive hall and featuring surviving costumes, furniture, porcelain, a sedan chair, musical instruments and other relics of the imperial reign.

Imperial Tombs

The tombs of the Nguyen emperors lie some way out of town — the nearest of them is seven kilometers from the city center. If you're on a package tour, it'll include most of them and, like the imperial tombs outside Beijing, you'll be dragged from one to the other until you drop. If you hire a bicycle and go there on your own, you can be selective about what you want to see, and there really are only three locations that inspire real interest. The **Tomb of Tu Duc**, who ruled from 1848 to 1883, is among the closest, located in **Duong Xuan Thuong village** about seven kilometers from town. Inside an octagonal stone wall, the monarch's sepulcher lies alongside a small lake surrounded by a pavilion, temple, honor courtyard lined with stone sculptures of elephants, horses and mandarins and a stele pavilion sheltering a 20-tonne stone tablet recording Tu Duc's virtues and triumphs.

The **tomb of Khai Dinh**, who ruled from 1916 to 1925, reflects how Westernized even the imperial court had become by then — the architecture and statues have vague European characteristics. The stele pavilion is in the middle of the traditional honor courtyard, with its guardian beasts and mandarins, and an image of Khai Dinh himself sits under a concrete canopy in the complex's ornate main hall, its walls decorated with elaborate frescoes. The most impressive tomb, that of **Emperor Minh Mang** (1820–1840), lies 12 km (seven and a half miles) from Hue at **An Bang** on the

Perfume River. Three great ceremonial gates and three granite staircases lead to the stele pavilion. Three terraces then lead to Sung An Temple, dedicated to the emperor and his empress. Three bridges cross the tiny Lake of Impeccable Clarity, the central one made of marble and used only by the emperor. Finally, three more terraces representing Heaven, Earth and Water provide the foundation for another magnificent building, the Minh Lau Pavilion. Minh Mang's burial mound lies inside a circular wall representing the sun at the top of a stone staircase flanked by sculptured dragons.

Thien Mu Pagoda

There is no other place of worship in Vietnam in such a beautiful location — this

renowned seven-storey octagonal tower and adjacent prayer hall perched on a promontory right over one of the most dramatic sections of the Perfume River. The view is wonderful — the river widening and stretching through green pastures and paddies toward misty blue mountains. The pagoda was founded in 1601, but the present tower was built by Emperor Thieu Tri in 1844. Adjacent to the tower, in a two-storey pavilion, there's a giant bell which was cast in 1710 and which the monks will toll for you if you ask them. They say you can hear its boom up to 10 km (six miles) away. There's also an Austin car, of all things, behind the main hall. It was used to take the bonze Thich Quang to Saigon in 1963 — where he was one of the Buddhist martyrs who burned himself to death in protest against the Diem regime. You'll come across several temples in Hue, but I can honestly assure you that the Thien Mu Pagoda is the one to see.

Notre Dame Cathedral

You'll see the strange spire of Notre Dame poking up over the skyline the moment you arrive in Hue, and you'll marvel at it. The cathedral is a grand but somewhat bizarre blend of European and Vietnamese architecture, and the spire is distinctly Asian. Actually, Notre Dame Cathedral was built as late as 1962, but what it lacks in history it certainly

The Linh Mu Pagoda in Hue, overlooking the Perfume River.

makes up for in appearance. To visit it, you go to 80 Nguyen Hue Street.

WHERE TO STAY

Most tour groups are taken straight to the **Huong Giang Hotel (℃ (54) 2122)** which is right on the bank of the Perfume River at 51 Le Loi Street, facing across to Hue's central market. It's a rather severe hotel, with a lobby full of backbreaking traditional rosewood furniture and upstairs hallways that remind you of a secondary school during classes.

But the rooms are air-conditioned, equiped with mosquito nets and have balconies from which you can enjoy the Huong Giang's biggest asset — its panoramic view of the river and bustling sampan communities. It also has a ground-floor restaurant terrace where you can sit at night and watch the battery-driven TV sets flickering under the woven bamboo canopies of the boats. In early 1993, the Huong Giang was charging US$42 a night for a double room. A new annex was reaching completion right next door.

ABOVE: Sampan and harvested bamboo on the Perfume River. OPPOSITE: Minh Manh Tomb in the imperial burial grounds outside Hue.

Elsewhere, the **Chinh Phu Hotel**, south along the riverbank at 5 Le Loi Street, is a rather stately villa which was once the palace of the governor of Central Vietnam. Its room rates are about the same as the Huong Giang's. The **Thuan Hoa Hotel (℃ (54) 2576)**, close to the Huong Giang at 7B Nguyen Tri Phuong Street, is another attractive establishment catering for foreigners.

WHERE TO EAT

The Huong Giang Hotel has two fairly good restaurants serving Vietnamese and Chinese food — its riverside patio and a fourth floor dining room. But there are more enjoyable venues in Hue. For instance, you can dine over the river at the **Song Huong Floating Restaurant, ℃ (54) 3738**, just south of the Huong Giang where Le Loi Street intersects with Hung Vuong Street. You can eat in the Citadel at the **Huong Sen Restaurant (℃ (54) 3201)**, which is a pavilion-style establishment set over a lotus pond. Or you can inquire at the Huong Giang Hotel or the city's two tourism authorities, **Hue Province Tourism (℃ (54) 2369)** located in the hotel grounds, or **Hue City Tourism (℃ (54) 3577)** at 18 Le Loi Street, about **hiring a sampan** with a traditional orchestra and singers and enjoying a dinner cruise along the river in the still of the night. The boat will cost about US$40, and the food comes extra.

GETTING THERE

Vietnam Airlines operates regular services from Saigon, Hanoi and Danang to Hue's Phu Bai Airport about 17 km (10.5 miles) south of the city. But again, the most enjoyable way to get there is by road from Danang, 108 km (67 miles) to the south. The trip takes about four hours—six if you allow for photo-stops and lunch — and it takes you through some of Vietnam's most scenic countryside. The road switchbacks through three high mountain passes interspersed with coastal farmland, fishing hamlets and a couple of vast agricultural plains set around wide bays. Once in Hue, you should be able to hire bicycles, and I suggest you check this out with the Huong Giang and other major hotels.

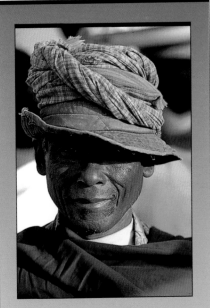

Cambodia

CAMBODIA is the wild card of travel and tourism in Indo-China. With the country divided into United Nations-protected enclaves and large, mainly northern areas occupied by the Khmer Rouge, access beyond Phnom Penh and Angkor (Siem Reap) is limited, and security even in these two government-controlled centers has been threatened by KR terrorism and organized military offensives.

For Cambodia, the Indo-China War hasn't ended — or rather, there's possibly one more war to go. The Vietnamese military withdrawal in 1990, forced by the United States and its allies as a prime condition for renewed diplomatic contacts with Hanoi, allowed the Khmer Rouge to sweep back into the country from their refugee bases inside the Thai border. Raising their banner of revolutionary nationalism once again, the guerrillas quickly grabbed control of most of the country beyond the capital and the Angkor ruins and began massacring ethnic Vietnamese communities, most of which had been established in Cambodia for many generations, reflecting the region's historical links with Vietnam's Mekong Delta.

With the Vietnamese military pullout, the United States and the four other permanent members of the United Nations Security Council cobbled together a program for peace and reconstruction in Cambodia in which the Khmer Rouge and other major resistance factions would disarm, canton their troops and prepare for democratic elections. The indefatigable Prince Norodom Sihanouk was installed at the head of a Supreme National Council which would administer the country while preparations were made for the national poll — but up until May 1993, when the elections were held, he spent most of his time under "medical supervision" in Beijing, relying on huge portraits of himself mounted on the Royal Palace and other strategic spots in Phnom Penh to remind everyone that he was once again the country's head of state. A force of more than 35,000 United Nations troops and military and civilian advisers was deployed to organize the elections and supervise an entire infrastructural and governmental reconstruction in Phnom Penh and other "safe"

areas. But the Khmer Rouge, firmly ensconced throughout the country and running a lucrative business in lumber and gems with the neighboring Thais, refused to disarm or have anything to do with the elections or the peace program; and by the time the elections were held they were not just kidnaping and attacking United Nations personnel in up-country bases but had launched a major offensive against Siem Reap that had halted tourism to the Angkor ruins.

This division and confrontation reflects many tiers of tragedy which exist in Cam-

bodia today. Since Richard Nixon widened the Vietnam War into Cambodia in 1970 to interdict the Ho Chi Minh Trail and buy time at the Paris peace talks, the country has been ravaged by bombing and counter-guerrilla warfare, plunged into the retributive horror of the Khmer Rouge "killing fields" — the genocidal purge in which more than a million people were murdered — then occupied by Vietnamese forces and now faces the prospect of becoming the Cyprus of Southeast Asia. But the most tragic aspect of all is that the country is beautiful, its people

OPPOSITE: Cambodian national flag flies from Foreign Affairs Ministry in Phnom Penh. ABOVE: Traditional music and dance are staged for visitors at the School of Fine Arts near the National Museum.

perhaps the friendliest and most exotic of Indo-China; and, were it not for the specter of the so-called "Marxist" Khmer Rouge and their grip on so much of the society, Cambodia would be a delightful and culturally fascinating high point of any Indo-China tour.

In mid-1993, you could certainly still travel there. Phnom Penh was safe, heavily protected by government and UNTAC (United Nations Transitional Assistance Command) forces, and quite easily accessible by air from Bangkok. But by this time, organized tourism to Angkor had ceased, placing Cambodia's most famed cultural attraction — and one of the world's wonders — off-limits to foreigners. The May elections saw more than 80 percent of the people in the United Nations enclaves turn out to vote, and a complete lack of Khmer Rouge reprisal had everyone from the UNTAC commander down declaring the poll a huge success. However, the fact that it coincided with the region's wet season, when torrential rains and flooding have been a traditional bar to serious military activity — and probably deterred the Khmer Rouge — was universally ignored.

The people of "free" Cambodia voted the royalist party, Funcinpec, into power, narrowly outpolling the governing Cambodian People's Party (CPP). Prince Sihanouk immediately sprang to full health in Beijing and flew back to be installed as head of state. But a bitter dispute between the two factions, with the CPP accusing the United Nations of ignoring alleged voting irregularities which had given Funcinpec an unfair advantage, threatened to boil into violence once the dry season set in; and there was little doubt in anyone's mind that if fighting broke out, the Khmer Rouge would take advantage of it to extend its grip on the country. Until the tension at that time resolved itself, whether to a return to divided status quo or a concerted drive by government and United Nations forces to break the Khmer Rouge stranglehold, it required the eminent prudence of anyone planning to travel to Cambodia to study the situation there first.

ABOVE: Archar Mean Boulevard, Phnom Penh's chaotic main street.

PHNOM PENH

The energy and clamor of the Cambodian capital makes even Saigon look somewhat sedate, and a lot of it has to do with its struggle to resurrect itself from the excesses of "Year Zero." In 1990, I saw some Vietnamese archive footage of Phnom Penh, taken when their invasion forces entered the capital in 1979. It was a ghost city, completely deserted — not a soul to be seen in its streets, its commercial buildings and temples left to fall into decay, the scenes made all the more deathly by the fact that they'd been shot on black-and-white film. The Khmer Rouge had literally closed the city down, emptying it of virtually all its people and marching

them off to the killing fields or forced labor in the countryside.

Today, Phnom Penh is booming again with life and commerce. Its long boulevards and narrow sidestreets are packed with traffic, a constant day-long tumult of cars, motorbikes, cyclos and bicycles with UN-TAC jeeps and trucks battling for right-of-way in the melee. Like the other capitals of Indo-China, its shops and markets are full of imported goods — the latest TVs and hi-fis, cameras, watches, perfumes and all manner of other luxuries, along with Thai jewelry and fashions and cheap factory clothing from China.

New investment has poured in, mainly into new hotels, restaurants and bars catering for UNTAC personnel and a growing in-flux of business travelers from Hong Kong, Taiwan and Thailand looking for low-cost joint-venture property and manufacturing deals. When I was there, the huge Cambodiana Hotel and nearby Phnom Penh Floating Hotel were virtually booked out and charging up to US$180 a night for a standard room. Daily Thai Airways and Cambodian International Airlines flights from Bangkok were feeding a steady flow of tourists, most of them on mandatory group packages, into five-night tours of Phnom Penh and Angkor; and Hong Kong's Dragonair was planning to launch a scheduled service in association with the national carrier.

In a sense, Phnom Penh is the capital most reminiscent of old Indo-China — all this development and business going on

in a city whose infrastructure has fallen too far behind to cope. It's given it a certain excitement and decrepit charm — most of its old French architecture virtually falling apart before the eyes, its teeming sidestreets badly potholed and forcing traffic into a state of blaring, elbowing anarchy that reminded me of Saigon in the late 1960s. With almost every service and utility — water supply, power, sanitation and communications — blowing gaskets trying to keep up with the boom, a key element of the UNTAC mandate is to help rebuild everything from an uninterrupted electricity system to a reasonably efficient government bureaucracy and maintain security at the same time, just as the Americans were doing during the war in Vietnam.

I found the people of Phnom Penh to be warm, overtly friendly and, apart from the Chinese merchants, quite guileless; and there's a reason for this. With most of the urban middle class wiped out by the Khmer Rouge, the city was repopulated with rural folk when the Vietnamese liberated it, and a lot of them haven't yet inherited the blase sophistication of the past. I found the city to be freer and more wide open than Hanoi, Saigon and Vientiane — freer in everything from black market currency exchange to open contact with the people — and there was a reason for this, too. As a Canadian pilot aboard my Cambodian Air flight from Bangkok put it: "The society's being rebuilt from the bottom up. There are no rules — it hasn't got time for them. The rules will come later when everything's in place." I remember musing over this when I visited one of the city's most popular up-market restaurants, La Paillote on the edge of the Central Market, where a sign on the door read: "Please refrain from smoking marijuana on these premises." And at Le Royal disco at the Royal (formerly Samaki) Hotel, packed out nightly with young prostitutes from Vietnam, most of them straight out of the rice paddies and tottering and stumbling about in their first high-heels.

Phnom Penh is a fairly easy place to get around, especially if you hire a motorcycle at US$10 a day (24 hours) and head where you please. The city lies north-south along the left bank of the Tonle Sap River, right at the confluence of this waterway, the Mekong and the Bassac — beyond which they all start to sprawl into the Mekong Delta of southern Vietnam. The most important boulevards all run north-south, too, so that the riverbank and its long thoroughfare Quai Karl Marx (a legacy of the Khmer Rouge reign and probably soon to be renamed) provide a reference point for all other areas. The main street is Achar Mean Boulevard, and as it runs south it passes Phnom Penh's derelict railway station, its flamboyantly domed new Central Market and most of the leading hotels — the imposing old Royal, where the foreign press were holed up during the Khmer Rouge takeover

of the city, the Mittapheap, Pailin, Singapore, Paradis, Dusit and Sukalay — before reaching the Cambodiana and Floating hotels and the Royal Palace.

The Central Market looks a bit like a domed mosque without minarets, and has a cavernous main hall where you can buy jewelry, gems and watches, surrounded by lanes of open stalls selling everything from vegetables to UNTAC T-shirts and music cassettes. It's the center of town, and another good reference point for urban navigation, and it's surrounded by textile stores, restau-

rants (including La Paillote), "black market" currency exchange dealers and, if it's still there, a political party headquarters with a banner declaring "Communism is Evil."

At first glance, the city is derelict, seedy and an uninspiring blend of decrepit French commercial buildings and graceless concrete tenements. Aside from the Royal Palace, which is said to have been designed to rival that of the Thai monarchy in Bangkok, a couple of temples, the Cambodiana Hotel complex and the renovated French villas in the old embassy district on Boulevard Tousamuth, there isn't really that much to see. That's if you want an orthodox sightseeing visit. But if you want to touch the soul of modern-day Phnom Penh, it is the people who make a visit here so memorable, and the warmth and spontaneity they seem to be able to exhibit against the dark backdrop of the city's other prime attractions — the dreadful relics of "Year Zero."

ABOVE: A garish new Central Market building marks the downtown hub of Phnom Penh.

WHAT TO SEE

The Royal Palace

The Royal Palace's opulently decorated main gate and watchful portrait of Prince Sihanouk face Lenin Boulevard (another legacy of the Khmer Rouge) and a large open park leading to a paved promenade along the river. It's an inviting edifice, with glittering temple spires rising above its walls and sweeping tiled roofs, and the whole complex definitely reminiscent of the Grand

Palace in Bangkok, on which it was modeled. The trouble is, you may not be able to get into it. The palace is supposed to be open to public visits on Thursdays and Sundays, but this seems to depend on the state of security in the city; and with Sihanouk now officially back in residence, and political unrest threatening in the wake of the elections, you may find that visits at any time are barred.

The palace's **Throne Hall** and **Silver Pagoda** are its most treasured attractions. Although most of its relics were destroyed by the Khmer Rouge, the Throne Hall, crowned with a 59-m-high stupa similar to the towers of the Bayon Temple in Angkor, recalls something of the wealth and splendor of the Khmer civilization. Amid wall and ceiling murals of the *Ramayana*, you'll find several thrones, including a gilded contraption in which the king was carried at royal processions. In the nearby King's

ABOVE: Cyclo driver on Phnom Penh's Lenin Boulevard. OPPOSITE: Main gate at the Royal Palace, official residence of King Norodom Sihanouk.

Pavilion, watched over by four garudas, there are two more modest sedan chairs which the monarch and his queen presumably used for less official public appearances, rather like using the Toyota to go shopping instead of the Rolls.

The Silver Pagoda

The Silver Pagoda, or **Wat Preah Keo** (Emerald Buddha Pagoda) is probably Cambodia's most priceless treasure. Its floor is laid with more than 5,000 solid silver tiles, and the Emerald Buddha itself, is displayed on a dais surrounded by several gold Buddha images encrusted with diamonds. Another huge mural of the *Ramayana* decorates a wall which runs right around the temple complex. Around the pagoda you'll find statues of Cambodia's most recent monarchs, a ceremonial bell tower, various monuments donated by such historical figures as Napoleon III and a pavilion displaying a bronze footprint of the Buddha from Sri Lanka.

National Museum

Across the road from the palace's northern wall, the National Museum is housed in a similarly inviting ocher-colored classical building constructed in 1917. Open daily from Tuesday to Sunday, it features Khmer paintings and sculpture dating back to the pre-Angkor states of Funan and Chenla, and its School of Fine Arts, located behind the main building, often stages performances of traditional Khmer music and dance. But the whole complex is badly run down, with parts of it undergoing renovation, and unless you go there with a local guide you'll spend a great deal of time simply finding someone with the authority to let you in. Just up the street from the museum, a long string of old shophouses has been transformed into a sort of open college for foreign language students.

Phnom Penh's main temples

While the Khmer Rouge spared the Royal Palace from complete destruction, Phnom Penh's main temples weren't so lucky. **Wat Ounalom**, at the corner of Lenin Boulevard and 154 Street, was literally torn apart during Year Zero and is now being restored. It

features a stupa which is said to contain a hair from an eyebrow of the Buddha, and a marble Buddha image which was smashed to pieces by the KR; but while this is an important Buddhist institute, it has no historical significance: it was built as recently as 1952. **Wat Lang Ka**, located close to the Victory Monument (built in 1958 to celebrated Cambodian independence) is another temple which was ravaged by the Khmer Rouge but is now restored and has a small community of monks back in residence. The Victory monument is now a

memorial to servicemen who lost their lives in the Vietnamese-led liberation of Cambodia in 1979.

Wat Phnom is a distinctly historical place —located on a hillock north of the city center and reportedly built in 1373 to commemorate a woman named Penh who discovered four Buddha images washed there by the river. Hence Phnom Penh — the "Hill of Penh." This stupa and surrounding shrines and pavilions were also virtually destroyed by the Khmer Rouge, and there's not much of interest at the site now except its proximity to the walled main compound and com-

mand headquarters of UNTAC, just across the street. **Wat Koh**, situated off Achar Mean Boulevard at 17 Street, and **Wat Moha Montrei**, which you'll find near the National Sports Stadium to the southwest of the city center, are two other temples which have been rebuilt since the 1975–79 extermination.

Boeng Kak Amusement Park

The Boeng Kak Amusement Park lies alongside a wide lake off Achar Mean Boulevard at 80 Street, but don't expect a Khmer version of Coney Island. It's a rather pathetic collection of derelict fairground rides, including a rusted ferris wheel, and the stripped fuselage of a United States helicopter and single-engine reconnaissance plane which have become playthings for local children. The park features two lakeside seafood restaurants, but you can get quite depressed here, mindful of the cultural poverty that still underscores Phnom Penh's drive to triumph over the ravages of Year Zero.

Tuol Sleng Museum

With this in mind, it's hardly surprising that the city's two most dramatic monuments are those connected with the darkness and brutality of that time.

One is the Tuol Sleng Museum, formerly Tuol Svay Prey High School, which the Khmer Rouge turned into Security Prison 21 — their main detention, interrogation and torture center for class enemies during Year Zero. It's a bleak collection of old school buildings surrounded by a tall fence topped with barbed wire on 113 Street, west of Achar Mean Boulevard, and although a lot of its most hideous features — the various instruments of torture — have been removed, it still chills the heart when you try to imagine the suffering and despair of the thousands of people who passed through this charnel house. What is even more shocking is a vast gallery of small passport-size photos of the detainees, exhibited on wall after wall within the main buildings, and their ages—condemned to death before interrogation and most of them are little more than teen-agers, stunned and completely helpless, in the grip of a regime that was all the more insane for the grim efficiency with which it recorded its purge.

ABOVE: Elaborate bas-relief at Wat Phnom in Phnom Penh. OPPOSITE: Spires of Wat Botum.

The Killing Fields

From there, a visit to Phnom Penh leads inevitably to the killing fields itself — or rather, one of the many mass execution spots that operated throughout Cambodia during the Khmer Rouge reign. You get to the former extermination camp of **Choeung Ek** via Pokambar Boulevard, which sweeps southwest from Achar Mean and the Central Market to the edge of the city, then turns left into tranquil rice fields and small farming communities. This trip is such a perverse contrast of rural industry, happy-go-lucky children who shout "Hello-goodbye!" as you ride past, tall, haughty russet colored brahmin cattle hauling traditional rice-carts and the horror that awaits you at Choeung Ek. There, about 15 km (nine miles) from the city, a tall glass-faced monument contains nearly 9,000 skulls, the remains of victims dug from mass graves nearby, the grim relics arranged in tier upon tier up the tower according to sex and age.

No amount of description can really prepare anyone for these two monuments. Yet in a way they represent the triumph of Phnom Penh and Cambodia — for when you finally leave them and travel back into the sudden warmth, friendliness and exuberance of the society, you realize that, for all their poverty, it is the people of Phnom Penh who make the city such a fascinating and different travel destination, and you can only marvel at the way they laugh and bustle about their business with such a terrible shadow hanging over their past.

WHERE TO STAY

Phnom Penh has many hotels, a lot of them constructed or renovated especially for UNTAC personnel, who enjoyed a daily hardship per diem of US$142 until the United Nations withdrew it in 1993. Room availability immediately improved, and rates fell slightly. Although the Cambodiana and Floating Hotel are high-priced, touting themselves as the only real international-class business hotels in Phnom Penh, most of the smaller properties have fax and telephone services, CNN/Star-Plus satellite services either in the lobby or individual rooms, a reasonable breakfast and rates in the US$30 to US$45 range.

The **Phnom Penh Floating Hotel** isn't anything like its custom-built counterpart in Saigon — it's a genuine seagoing vessel that's been converted and renovated as a hotel. That adds a certain novelty to it, but you may find there's something about the configuration of the lobby area and bars that makes it cold and uncomfortable. You can also feel the vibration of the generators through the steel decks. It does have a large restaurant and coffee shop, the Battambang. Otherwise, it's been so successful, with 90 to 95 percent occupancy most of the time, and rates in the US$150 to

US$180 range, that a second 150-room floating palace was due to join it in late 1994 to form what its owners envisage as Phnom Penh's premier hotel and entertainment center.

The Sofitel-managed **Hotel Cambodiana** has a main wing of 360 rooms surrounded by restaurants, bars, shops, garden bistros and chalets, all set on the bank of the Tonle Sap. It's a grand palace of a hotel, which took from 1967 to 1987 to build, the construction halted for years by warfare and the Khmer Rouge purge. This is the place to stay if you want absolute comfort and all facilities, but expect to pay around $200 a night in a setting and ambience which could have been a four-star property in Bangkok.

For a much more satisfying taste of old Indo-China, at a fraction of the price, the **Renakse Hotel**, opposite the southern end of the Royal Palace complex and just a few blocks away from the Cambodiana, is highly

OPPOSITE: The five-star Cambodiana Hotel and pool TOP. BOTTOM The nearby Phnom Penh Floating Hotel. ABOVE: Skulls pack the macabre shrine to Pol Pot's victims at Choeung Ek.

recommended. This former Buddhist institute has small rooms with temperamental air-conditioning and charges US$35 to US$40 a night, but its lobby is an open, tiled verandah that looks out on to gardens of frangipani trees and, on the right night, the moon rising over the temple spires of the Royal Palace. The food is fairly basic—Continental breakfast and snacks (noodle dishes and French baguettes) for the rest of the day —but the coffee is good, and staff friendly and accommodating and you can enjoy BBC World Service on the lobby TV in the evening.

opulent and comfortable, has a more efficient standard of service and charges US$60 to US$75 a night. You'll find it on 234 Street N°130 opposite the Central Market.

Further north, the **Hotel Royal** looks fascinating from the outside, with its ornate French facade, and the role it played during the Khmer Rouge takeover gives it a certain mystique. But once inside, it is dingy and in need of a good renovation, and its nightly disco attracts hundreds of young Vietnamese prostitutes. While this may not worry some guests, it also means that the Royal's

Uptown, close to the Central Market, the **Pailin Hotel** at 219 Achar Mean Boulevard profits from its central location and has a good second-floor restaurant. But its rooms are sparsely furnished for the price—US$70 to US$90 a night—and the staff don't really care if you stay there or not. There's a TV set in every room, but it's tuned only to Canal France International, which seems to feature a lot of game shows.

Close by, the **Sukalay**, **Mittapheap** and **Monorom** hotels offer a similar decor and service, with rates ranging from US$40 to US$65 a night depending on the class of room and whether it has a bathroom and hot water. The **Hotel La Paillote**, home of the restaurant of the same name, is a little more

main clientele are Korean, Japanese and Taiwanese businessmen with one thing on their mind besides business. Room rates are around US$40 for a standard single to US$50 for a Grand Bungalow in the garden.

Finally, the **Guest House Hirondelle** on the riverfront at 79 Quai Karl Marx should not be confused with Phnom Penh's mainstream hospitality. Its chief service is "massage & steam bath."

WHERE TO EAT

With UNTAC personnel from no less than 31 countries based in and around Phnom Penh, it should come as no surprise to find a wide variety of restaurants to choose from.

At the top of the line, the Thai-owned **La Paillote** at 234 Street Nº130 (€ (23) 22151) caters to the cream of the UNTAC and diplomatic communities with excellent French and Continental cuisine, plus Thai favorites, at very pleasant prices — a meal for four with dessert and coffee at about US$10 a head.

La Mousson at 55 Street Nº178 (€ (23) 27250) is also recommended, but its chicly renovated premises in an old villa near the Royal Palace says a lot for its service — it's more expensive and rather snobbish compared with La Paillote. La Mousson also

MTV and local pop videos while you're trying to chat and eat.

Alongside these quality restaurants, you'll find several up-market bars which also serve meals and are set up specifically for UNTAC personnel, foreign businesspeople and tourists. The **No Problem Cafe** is one of them — others are the **Gecko Bar** and the obviously copy-cat **Rock Hard Cafe**. They're both very pleasant retreats from the dust, dereliction and pandemonium of Phnom Penh, but they're also quite pretentious and expensive. The Hong Kong-owned Gecko Bar features lots

operates the No Problem cafe, one of Phnom Penh's expatriate in-places which is similarly chic and charges US$5 for a cappuchino coffee.

The **Paris Pizza and Cocktail Bar** at 433 Achar Mean Boulevard is another surprise — it has the best Italian food in town, along with "homemade firewood pizza and French food." As for Thai food in an up-market setting, the **Chao Pra Ya**, set up in another restored villa at 67 Boulevard Tousamuth (€ (23) 22759) is as good as anything in Bangkok and will set you back about US$8 to US$10 a head. It has a main restaurant and garden barbecue and attentive waiters, and if there's anything that could be said against the decor and service it's the TV that blares

of mirrors, heavy inlaid Oriental furniture and picture frames around its air- conditioners, and charges US$5 for a spaghetti Bolognaise. At the Rock Hard Cafe, a steak sandwich is US$5, a screwdriver is US$5.50 ("You don't pay that for a screwdriver anywhere," I heard a visitor from San Francisco complain), souvenir T-shirts are US$10, souvenir Zippos are US$20 and the cocktail list features such delights as B-52, Panty Dropper and Slippery Nipple. That's the sort of place it is.

Below these establishments, there are dozens of smaller bars, most of them locally

OPPOSITE: The No Problem and Mousson pub and restaurant in Phnom Penh. ABOVE: Hand-woven silks and other traditional textiles can be found in shops ringing the Central Market.

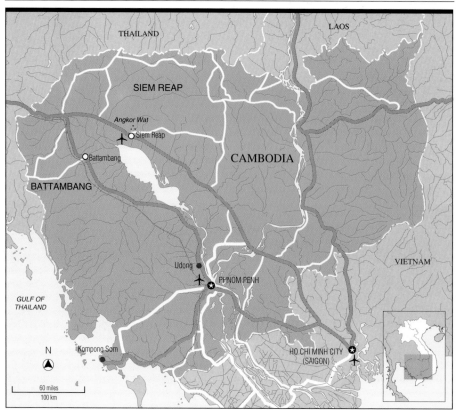

owned, where you can get a cold beer at market prices — US$1 a can or bottle — and enjoy a cheap but good quality snack or meal. The **Cherry Tree** on Rue 126 opposite Express Tour Co near the Central Market is one such place, and there's another clean, friendly bar called the **Bus Stop** close to the UNTAC headquarters compound north of the city center.

Local restaurants are mainly Chinese-owned and serve a variety of Chinese and Cambodian dishes. My favorite is the **Ponloik**, an informal double-storey establishment which you'll find on the riverfront just north of the Royal Palace, where you can enjoy an excellent meal of deep fried pepper prawns, roast chicken and braised fish for about US$7 a head. Another popular place is the **Chez Lipp**, located just off the northern stretch of Achar Mean Boulevard near the Boeng Kak amusement park. Here, in a rustic open pavilion with faded travel posters pinned to the walls, you'd be hard pressed to spend more than US$4 a head on a four-course meal including fish soup, beer and coffee; and the quality of the food is consistently good.

UDONG

One of the very few journeys you can make beyond Phnom Penh is to a hilltop complex of temples and stupas at Udong, about 45 km (28 miles) north of the city, which was the capital of Cambodia from 1618 to 1866. Tour agencies will take you there by car, or you can get there by motorbike — but either way, it's a long hard drive along a road that's in poor condition and on which the traffic knows no law. Once there, you're witness to more of the Khmer Rouge's cultural atrocities — the main temple of **Vihear Preah Chaul Nipean** was demolished during Year Zero, and its main relic, a huge sitting Buddha, blown to pieces. Nearby, three huge stupas, decorated with *garudas*, elephants and ceramic motifs, stand untouched, even though they commemorate three of the country's kings. From these stupas you look across a vast rice plain, contemplating once again the chilling juxtaposition of darkness and restoration in Cambodia: below the hill there's a memorial to victims recovered from more than 100 mass graves in the region.

KOMPONG SOM

This town on the south coast, about four hours from Phnom Penh by car, was Cambodia's main port before Year Zero and is struggling to regain its importance. Formerly called Sihanoukville, it's touted as a resort town with "superb beaches and shoals and reefs teeming with multicolored fish." Like

me, you'll have to accept that with a grain of salt. For now, a more accurate description is that Kompong Som may one day become an important access to virtually untouched islands, and their resort potential, that lie off the coast. In the meantime, its own beaches are hardly resort quality, its hotels are booked solidly throughout the year by Phnom Penh-based United Nations and corporate expatriates, and until the security situation improves it can be something of a hazard to get to. The highway from Phnom Penh passes through several government (CPP) armed checkpoints, manned by teen-age soldiers who can get trigger-happy if a vehicle approaches at high speed, and other areas where Khmer Rouge guerrillas are known to be in

control, especially after dark. What's perhaps more off-putting is that it also takes you through one of Cambodia's prime logging areas, with depots and sawmills lining its sides for many kilometers, and you are given a depressing picture of the extent to which the country's forests are being raped. On my own trip, we were unable to get into the town's sole beachside guesthouse and decided to head back to Phnom Penh. Our driver became very agitated, trying to hurry us through our lunch before we left. I asked him why he was getting so

nervous. He ran a finger across his throat and pointed at his watch. "After four o'clock," he said, "Pol Pot."

ANGKOR

This vast, mostly ruined complex of Hindu-Khmer temples, the legacy of the Khmer Empire, is what draws most visitors to Cambodia. And on the whole, none of them are disappointed, though visions of one of the

ABOVE: Newly weds LEFT in Phnom Penh testify to Cambodia's arduous recovery from horror. RIGHT: Girl in traditional dress, Siam Reap. OVERLEAF: Stone causeway leads to the main entrance and architectural wonders of Angkor Wat.

world's great cultural wonders are tempered somewhat by the decay, damage and evident neglect of much of the site.

There are good reasons for this, of course. Angkor has been right in the theater of war in Cambodia since the Khmer Rouge first used it as a sanctuary during the United States-led offensive in Cambodia in the 1970s, figuring quite rightly that such an illustrious historical relic would be spared the carpet bombing and other operations that engulfed much of the rest of the country. Even though it's Cambodia's main tourist

revenue-earner, the Khmer Rouge still dominate the area today, as was illustrated just before the 1993 elections when a main force unit attacked the town of Siem Reap. Most of the temple sites were being guarded by government outposts at that time, and there were signs all over the place warning about minefields in the scrubland off the main tracks.

Even so, to visit Angkor is not just to step back into history, to the height of Khmer power in the seventh to eleventh centuries, but also to get about as close as you can to

PREVIOUS PAGE: Dawn over Angkor Wat — one of the eight great wonders of the world. ABOVE: Siam Reap's Grand Hotel, gateway to Angkor Wat. OPPOSITE: Angkor's main surviving ruins are still in the crossfire of government and Khmer Rouge troops.

what it must have felt to be an intrepid explorer or archaeologist at the turn of the century, stumbling across ruins in the jungle. Most of the minor temple sites are overgrown by the trees and undergrowth; others are off-limits because of mines or poor security. But the present package tour, fairly strictly enforced by the authorities and lasting virtually all day, will take you to the best relics that Angkor has to offer, including its three most famous attractions, **Angkor Wat**, the temple of **Bayon** and **Ta Prohm** with the **Baphnon**. The tour guides are also very accommodating, considering the money spinner that Angkor has become. They don't hustle you along from one spot to the next and are quite content to let you spend as long as you want at each site — as long as you're ready to head back to town by nightfall.

SIEM REAP

This, the main access point to the Angkor ruins, is a fairly idyllic little market town, dissected by a river, despite being a regular target of Khmer Rouge activity. It also has one of Cambodia's most famous hotels, the old **Grand Hotel d'Angkor**, where most tour groups are booked and where a comfortable high-ceilinged room with mosquito nets and a huge tiled bathroom is included in the package at about US$45 a night. In 1993 it was about to be renovated by a Thai hotel management company, though the work may have been put off by subsequent Khmer Rouge attacks on the town. The Grand has a very cozy bar, a dining room where the menu varies in quality and a small auditorium where performances of classical dance are staged each Friday and Saturday night.

Outside the Grand, several new hotels and guesthouses have sprung up to compete for tourists and also cater for United Nations personnel. The Grand operates one of them, the **Villa Apsara**, right across the street from the main hotel, with a pool and chalet-style rooms at US$55 a night. Another new property, **Golden Apsara Guesthouse** at 220 Mondol I, has rooms for US$10 to US$20, while the unfortunately named **Hotel Stung** on Wath Prom Rath Street charges US$50 to US$80. The renovated **Hotel de la**

Paix on Sivatha Street has hiked its rates up to between US$60 and US$90 a night.

Most visitors eat in their hotels, but there are several good restaurants and bars — most of them for locals and United Nations soldiers. The best place is the **Restaurant Samapheap**, with an open dining pavilion and garden, located just across the river from the Grand Hotel. Another popular spot is the **Ban Thai Guesthouse and Restaurant** which you'll find on the main road from the Grand to the Central Market, close to a sign which reads "United Nations Vehicle Wash-

enough, crowded with sculptures of apsaras and other Hindu carvings, but this in turn opens on to a vast courtyard that leads to the main temple itself. This gigantic three-storey structure, rising 55 m (180 ft) from the ground, was built by King Suryavarman II (1112–1152) and dedicated to Vishnu. Of all the monuments of Angkor, it is this great structure, quite apart from the wealth of bas-relief carvings of Hindu epics and Khmer battles adorning the walls and cloisters surrounding it, which testifies to the power and glory of the Khmer civilization.

ing Station & Tire Fix." The **Green House Kitchen**, on the road in from the airport, is a new Thai-style restaurant housed in a big pavilion.

THE TEMPLE TOUR

Angkor was the capital of the Khmer Empire, a vast city, and what you'll see today is only a fraction of its ancient splendor. Even so, **Angkor Wat** itself, the first stop on the temple tour, rivals the pyramids of Egypt for the monumental vision and artistry of its time. You approach the outer temple walls along a wide, dilapidated stone causeway that runs across what was once a protective moat. The main gate and its walls are spectacular

By contrast, the **temple of Bayon**, is smaller, more compact and has none of the great perspectives of Angkor Wat. Yet in many respects this is the most fascinating of all the Angkor monuments. Built in the reign of Jayavarman VII (1181–1201), it lies in a wide clearing in the forest which was once the epicenter of the city of Angkor Thom. Where Angkor Wat sheds an almost golden glow in the late afternoon sunlight, Bayon is granite gray, the stone of its walls, towers and stairways crumbled and pitted by time; yet its artistry arouses a sense of awe — its

OPPOSITE: The South Gate at Angkor Wat. ABOVE: Many artistic treasures, such as these incredible bas-reliefs, have survived Cambodia's years of conflict. OVERLEAF: Girls in traditional dress in Siam Reap.

upper level mounted by no less than 49 towers bearing 172 huge, Buddha-like faces of the god Avalokitesvara. Wherever you stand, these moon-like features are watching you, some of them so big that they fill your view, others barely recognizable within the stonework, so harshly have they been worn by elements. Elsewhere in the galleries and cloisters of this momentous relic, some 11,000 other carvings depict Hindu legends and Khmer life at that time.

Ta Prohm, with the **Baphuan** is the most derelict of all the Angkor temples, but the

Elephants, 350 m (1,150 ft) long and used as a Kremlin-style dais where the Khmer rulers reviewed their armies, is sculpted from one end to the other with bas-relief cavalry and war elephants. In the forest around the Bayon, huge ceremonial gates, all that remain of the precincts of Angkor Thom, have approaches lined with rows of sculptured guards — most of them now headless after centuries of looting and the latter-day damage wreaked by the Khmer Rouge.

An attempt has been made to halt the destruction and pillage at Angkor, and the

relic that most inspires the sense of intrepid discovery. Built as a Buddhist temple in the late Angkor period, it has been virtually reclaimed by the jungle, its stonework broken and heaved about by tree roots, as though an earthquake has struck it, and its passageways and cloisters piled with fallen masonry.

Elsewhere, monuments like **Ta Keo**, built by Jayavarman V (968–1001) in honor of Shiva, rise up out of the jungle in a series of lofty towers with huge stone steps that are exhausting to climb and must have instilled a sense of ignominy and dread in the worshipers of its day. The Terrace of the

Temple bas-reliefs ABOVE adorn the walls and niches alongside OPPOSITE huge Buddha faces at the awesome Bayong Temple.

Angkor Conservation Agency has managed to save about 5,000 statues and other relics, storing them in sheds at its compound between Siem Reap and Angkor Wat. When all this cultural treasure will be put back on display in the temples, God only knows — just as it is probably impossible at this time to judge when Angkor itself will be free of the political violence that holds it to ransom. With careful, expert renovation and a sustained period of peace, Angkor stands to become a cultural attraction and global treasure as precious as Borobudur in Indonesia. The same could almost be said of Cambodia itself, the continuing tragedy of Indo-China with the potential to become such a special highlight of any Indo-China tour.

Laos

THIS SLEEPY mountainous domain is, in many respects, the jewel of Indo-China. Where Vietnam faces dramatic economic and industrial development, with all the environmental problems that it will inevitably bring, and Cambodia struggles with its divisive political crisis, Laos promises several years yet of rustic, colorful serenity — a relatively mystical experience within the continuing upheaval of Indo-China. So much of this buffer state is undeveloped, comparatively undiscovered, virtually a mystery. So much of its French colonial character is still there, gracing its main cities and towns. So much of its spiritualism is still intact, its Buddhist temples flourishing, its festivals restoring vibrancy to its gentle culture, its people reaching back to traditions that have barely acknowledged nearly two decades of communist rule. Even the new Australian-funded bridge over the Mekong River, linking it directly with Thailand, promises little more than a symbolic step into modern Asia, making it possible to get directly to Vientiane by bus or car instead of the traditional Nong Khai river ferry.

That's not to say that Laos won't change. The bridge may well accelerate the rate at which the country is stripping its forests of timber for Thai entrepreneurs. The country remains threatened by the struggle between Thailand and Vietnam for economic and political dominance. Its relative poverty — poverty, that is, in relation to the industrial and trading growth of the rest of Southeast Asia — means that an industrial base of some sort must be developed soon if it is to compete with the rest of the region. But for the time being, to travel in Laos is to travel back to the more graceful days of Indo-China and the Buddhist traditions which have been corrupted by rapid economic growth in neighboring Thailand.

As elsewhere in this region, Laos has only two seasons, governed by the monsoons that bring rain and high humidity during the summer months from May to October and almost perfect conditions — warm and dry in the daytime, cool and dry at night — from November to April. However, as already mentioned, temperatures get more frigid, especially at night, in the northern mountains during the dry season.

Until about 1992, the only way to get into the country was by air from Bangkok, Saigon and Hanoi to Vientiane's Wattay International Airport. But you can now enter the way just about everyone did it in the days before the revolution, traveling by overnight train from Bangkok to Nong Khai, breakfasting on fried eggs and coffee on the bank of the Mekong and watching the border ferries chug to and fro, then making the short crossing to the Tha Deua customs and immigration post. If you're on a group or individual prepaid tour, as most visitors were when I

was there, you'll find a local tour agency mini-van or car waiting to take you the 20 km (12 miles) to Vientiane. If not, there are taxis available which will charge about US$5 to take you to town. Now, of course, there is there is the newly-built bridge as well.

You'll probably still only get a 15-day visa, whether arranged in Bangkok or elsewhere, and you must leave the country and apply for a new one if you wish to stay longer. If you overstay, you'll be fined US$5 for every day spent over the limit. At the time I visited, you needed special permits to travel beyond Vientiane and from one

OPPOSITE: Courtyard of Vientiane's Pha Tat Luang (Great Sacred Stupa). ABOVE: Stupa soars behind statue of King Setthathirat.

province to another, which meant you needed a local travel agency to arrange your tour; but this may have changed by now. It bears mentioning that I found the travel agencies in Vientiane, especially Raja Tour, which has its office at the Anou Hotel, extremely friendly, helpful and honest — reflecting, in fact, the general character of the Lao people.

You'll also find that United States dollars and Thai *baht* are accepted all over Laos as compatible currency with the local *kip*. The major credit cards are also accepted all over the place, notably American Express which was banned in Vietnam while the United States embargo remained in place. The only real problem when I was there was communication — getting an international telephone call or sending a fax — but this may well have improved since then. Whatever, Laos is a place where, once you're there, the rest of the world just isn't that important any more.

VIENTIANE

Vientiane, the Lao capital, has hardly changed since the days in the late 1960s when I used to go there each month from Bangkok to get my Thai visa renewed. It still has the character and feel of a large market town with an exotic veneer of French culture, an undercurrent of Buddhist sanctity, a bustle of largely ethnic Chinese trade and enterprise and a tendency to regard a traffic jam as a bank-up of too many bicycles. It has more than bicycles, of course, and in fact an astonishing stream of traffic — jeeps, Landcruisers, mini-buses, cars, motorcycles, pushbikes and pedal-cyclos — flows all day along the main street, Thanon Samsenthai, just as it did in the old days, leaving you to wonder whether it's not specially staged to give the town the appearance of urbanity.

The city lies along a broad curve of the Mekong, hugging the western bank, and most of its main streets like Thanon Samsenthai run parallel to the river. Others radiate to the north, like Thanon Lan Xang which is

a wide triumphal boulevard leading to the city's most incredible landmark, the towering Pratuxai Monument, which looks as though it was uprooted from somewhere in the vicinity of India's Taj Mahal. The city's tourist and business district begins in downtown Samsenthai, roughly where the Ekalath Metropole and Asia Pavilion hotels are, and extends southwest to the river, taking in an equally remarkable central fountain and nearby restaurants in Nam Phou Place and the waterfront Lan Xang Hotel. A second business district and sprawling retail area lies to the northwest along Thanon Samsenthai, centered on the Anou Hotel.

It's an easy city to deal with — compact, flat and with most major hotels, restaurants, agencies and attractions within walking distance of each other. Only when you head north to locations beyond Pratuxai Monument do you need transport, and then a bicycle or motorbike — both of which you can easily rent in Vientiane — are necessary.

WHAT TO SEE

The Temple Tour

Vientiane's prime cultural attraction is its temples, more than a dozen of them, headed in importance by the massive golden stupa,

ABOVE and OPPOSITE: Two views of Wat Si Muang, one of Vientiane's many well-preserved temples.

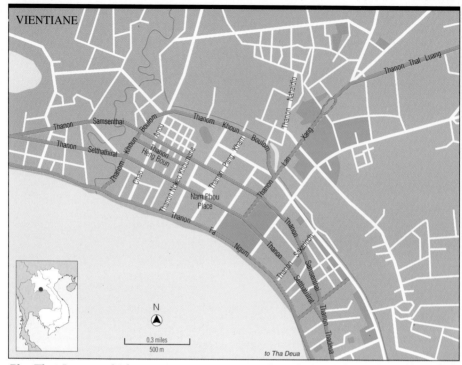

VIENTIANE

Thanon That Luang
Thanon Mahadio
Thanon Samsenthai
Thanon Khoun
Thanon Setthathirat
Thanon Khoun Boulom
Thanon Anou
Thanon Boulom
Thanon Heng Boun
Thanon Pang Kham
Thanon Xang
Thanon Lan
Nam Phou Place
Thanon Chao
Thanon Nokeo Khoumane
Thanon Fa
Ngum
Thanon
Thanon Sisangvone
Thanon Samsenthai
Thanon Setthathirat
Thanon Thadua

N

0.3 miles
500 m

to Tha Deua

Pha That Luang, which towers over two monasteries and walled cloisters four kilometers north of the city center at the end of Thanon That Luang. The most revered Buddhist monument in Laos, That Luang was built on the site of a Khmer temple by King Setthathirat in the mid-sixteenth century when Vientiane became the capital of the kingdom of Lan Xang. A statue of the founder sits atop a stone column in an enclosure in front of the huge timber main gates. That Luang was virtually destroyed in 1828 by invading Thais, and the present structure is the result of a French restoration in 1900. In November each year, the complex becomes the focus of Vientiane's biggest religious festival. On the first day, a sacred white elephant is led to the stupa while ritual processions celebrate the event at temples all over the city. Hundreds of monks and novices pour in from the provinces to take up a vigil in the cloisters around the stupa. At dawn on the second day, they're presented with alms and new robes. On the third day, thousands of Buddhist faithful

PREVIOUS PAGE: Sunset on the Mekong River in Vientiane. OPPOSITE: Ornately decorated entrance to main prayer hall at Wat Si Saket.

march on the stupa from the other temples, led by musicians and bearing offerings. Chanting and praying, they circle the stupa until the late hours of the night, many stopping to light candles and pray in the pandemonium.

Wat Si Saket is one of Vientiane's more splendid monasteries, and its oldest, located on a corner of the intersection where Thanon Lan Xang heads north from Thanon Setthathirat. Built in 1818, its architecture is very much Thai, while the inside walls of its cloister are packed with Lao-style Buddha images. A Khmer image of the Buddha seated under a canopy formed by a multi-headed cobra is one the the hall's showpieces, along with statues that were damaged in the war with the Thais in the early 1800s. The wat's main hall, also Thai-style, is lined with Buddhist murals and its ceiling is decorated with a floral design similar to those in the Thai temples of Ayutthaya.

Wat Pha Keo, just up Thanon Lan Xang from Wat Si Saket, was rebuilt in 1942 on the site of the former royal temple of the Lao kings. It's now a museum, with terraces and a main hall crowded with impressive

Buddha images dating back to the sixth century, along with a gilded throne and, in a garden to the rear of the hall, a stone jar from the Plain of Jars.

The name of **Wat Ong Teu Mahawihan**, located on Thanon Setthathirat near the intersection with Thanon Chao Anou, translates into Temple of the Heavy Buddha, dedicated to massive sixteenth century Buddha image made of bronze in its exquisitely decorated main hall.

Wat Si Muang, east of the city center at the confluence of Satthathirat and Samsen-

thai streets, is set in spacious grounds and is an ideal spot to sit and talk with the Laos as they come to pray and give offerings. A lot of people come here: one of the temple's most precious Buddha images, damaged in the war with the Thais, is said to have the power to grant wishes. Adjacent to the temple there's a public park dominated by a towering statue of King Sisavang Vong, who tried unsuccessfully to reconcile the French attempt to reclaim Laos in 1945 with a growing popular movement for independence.

Wat Sok Pa Luang and nearby **Wat Si Amphon**, south of the city center near the Mongolian Embassy, both offer something more than the usual temple tour. They provide soothing herbal saunas, administered

by nuns, and therapeutic massage if you require it. At Wat Sok Pa Luang there's also an elderly Thai monk who's an expert in Buddhist meditation and provides courses for foreigners, but speaks only Lao and Thai.

Buddha Park

This rather bizarre attraction is actually called **Wat Xieng Khwan**, but bears special mention because it's not a temple at all — it's a kind of showground, a Luna Park, of Buddhist and Hindu imagery set close to the Mekong south of Vientiane beyond the

Tha Deua border post. Crowded with just about every sacred image from the two religions that you can name, and dominated by a huge reclining Buddha, it would be reminiscent of a display of giant garden gnomes if the inspiration behind it wasn't so serious. It was designed and built in 1958 by a mystic named Luang Pu who founded a cult based on a mixture of Buddhist and Hindi theology. After the 1975 revolution he moved across the river to continue his teachings in Nong Khai. As strange as it is, Buddha Park is fascinating as a photo-opportunity as much as anything else — the various concrete figures are very well crafted — but whether you'll be similarly inspired is up to you.

Revolutionary Museum

The architecture of the old French mansion in which the Lao Revolutionary Museum is housed is one good reason for a visit. Another is a whole room devoted to a surprisingly professional exhibition of the history of the Russian Revolution — one of the last you'll see anywhere in the world, now that Soviet communism is in collapse. Other than that, this is a typical socialist revolutionary showplace, room after room of photo exhibits with an occasional weapon, uniform or revolutionary bust, designed

tribe silverwork, too, but you may also find that a lot of it is made in Thailand.

The City Tour

While it may well seem that Vientiane has little of interest to offer aside from temples, be assured that it has a special character well worth exploring. And the best way to do this is on a motorbike, which you can rent for about US$10 a day (24 hours) from a shop alongside the very helpful Inter-Lao Tourism office (℄ (21) 3134) on Setthathirat Street, just south of the fountain in Nam Phou

with little imagination and a lot of documentary clutter. You'll find the museum on Samsenthai Street, just over a block east of the Asia Pavilion Hotel.

Morning Market

This sprawling marketplace just north of the city center, to the right off Thanon Lan Xang, has cleaned up its image considerably since the height of the Vietnam War, when it had a whole section of stalls selling, among other things, various grades of marijuana. Today, much of the market has been moved into a series of huge pavilion-style buildings, and it's here that you'll find the souvenir Soviet military watches that I mentioned earlier in this book. You'll find Lao sarongs and hill-

Place. Bicycles are also available for hire, and Lao Tourism or your hotel desk will tell you where to get one.

Just cruising around the city will introduce you to its special contrast of colonial French and traditional Buddhist architecture; its people, who have a friendly dignity that's a shock after the more established tourist spots in Asia; its lifeline, the Mekong River, which is an adventure all its own if you follow the riverfront through a beehive of suburban communities that hug close to it on the western stretch toward the airport; and its rice fields and farming hamlets along

OPPOSITE and ABOVE: Vientiane Temple artistry.
OVERLEAF: Wat Xieng Khwang (Buddha Park) is Vientiane's "Disneyland" of Buddhist lore.

the southern road to Tha Deua and Buddha Park. It's a relaxing city, where you can quickly feel you've become immersed in the everyday life, yet still be excited at the prospect of new sights and encounters each day you set out.

WHERE TO STAY

The **Lan Xang Hotel** (((21) 3672) just back from the riverfront on Thanon Fa Ngum, is where most tour groups are booked. It's a comfortable hotel, but has that strict, imper-

Japanese tour groups. Most rooms have a fridge and TV, and rates for a double should still be in the US$40 area.

Le Parasol Blanc (((21) 9276) is a new distinctly up-market hotel, with chalet-style rooms set around a swimming pool, located in Thanon Nahaidio, a street running left off Thanom Lan Xang, just before the Pratuxai Monument. It's popular with consular and United Nations personnel, and charges about US$30 a night for a double room.

There are two quite deluxe Lani Guest-houses in Vientiane, both of them restored

sonal character of a typical socialist state-run operation and caters for a lot of official groups and cadres. But one thing it has going for it is a swimming pool, set among gardens and various caged wildlife — including two deer, a crocodile and a bear — at the rear. The pool gets crowded at weekends when local expatriates and their children are allowed in. The going rate for a standard double room was US$46 a night when I was there.

The **Asia Pavilion Hotel**, centrally located at 379 Samsenthai Street (((21) 3287), was a charmingly run-down French-owned establishment called the Constellation before the revolution. It's now been quite expensively renovated and caters for a lot of

villas in garden settings. **Lani One Guest-house** (((21) 4175) has 11 rooms and is at 228 Setthathirat Street, next to Wat Hay Sok, and you'll find **Lani Two** (((21) 2615) with seven rooms at 268 Thanom Saylom. Both charge about US$30 a night for a double.

The **Anou Hotel** (((21) 3324), in the western area of the city center at the intersection of Heng Boun and Chao Anou streets, is a particularly large establishment which was renovated in 1989. A double room costs about US$35 to US$40 a night, but beware of the hotel's main attraction, a nightclub which thumps out pop music until after midnight. The **Ekalath Metropole** (((21) 2881), a couple of blocks east of the Asia Pavilion on Samsenthai Street, has double rooms that are more like suites at US$35 a night, but its ground-floor Melody Bar can also keep you awake half the night. It's a friendly hotel, with a particularly good coffee shop, but in much need of renovation.

The **Santiphab Hotel** (℃ (21) 3305) at 69A Thanon Luang Prabang has the distinction of owning the only elevator in Vientiane. Rates are the same: about US$35 to US$40 a night. The **Ambassador Hotel** (℃ (21) 5797) on Thanon Pang Kham, which runs north past Nam Phou Place and the central fountain, rents its double rooms at US$60 a night.

by far the best. It also specializes in very good, authentic pizzas. Outside the hotels, the finest privately operated restaurant, by far, is the **Nam Phu** (℃ (21) 4723) in Nam Phou Place opposite the fountain. Its speciality is French cuisine, but will provide Lao food on demand, and it's very popular with visiting French tourists and officials, along with United Nations and aid agency expatriates. Right opposite Nam Phu, **L'Opera** is a new Italian restaurant, with an Italian chef, which becomes an ice cream parlor in the daytime.

For a hotel with a difference, you might like to try the **River View** (℃ (21) 9123) which looks right over the Mekong River on the western end of Fa Ngum Street, four blocks beyond the Santiphab Hotel. It's a clean, friendly hotel, with double rooms at US$33 a night. The trouble is, its rooms all have windows glazed with bathroom glass, so none of them have a view of the river.

WHERE TO EAT

The Lan Xang, Anou and Asia Pavilion hotels all have good restaurants serving Western and Lao food, but the alfresco restaurant and piano bar at Le Parasol Blanc is

Other French and Western establishments which I can recommend are the **Arawan** (℃ (21) 3977) at 474 Thanon Samsenthai, which also has a well-stocked *charcuterie*; the **Ban Tavanh** (℃ (21) 2737) at 49 Thanom Khoun Boulom; the **Souriya** (℃ (21) 4411) at 31 Thanon Pang Kham; and the **Restaurant Santisouk** also known as **La Pagode** (℃ (21) 3926) on Thanon Nokeo Khoumane, which is a main street running north from the river to the Ekalath Metropole Hotel.

Two pub-style restaurant/bars are the **Kaonhot** (℃ (21) 3432) on Thanon Sakarindh, which specializes in grills and has a billiard

ABOVE: French bread alfresco and shoppers at the Morning Market. OPPOSITE: Asia Pavilion Hotel (formerly the Constellation) in downtown Vientiane.

room and disco, and **Somchan's Pub and Restaurant** (ℂ (21) 5563) which serves Lao food with the beer and has live music. Two other dining spots with a difference bear special mention: the **Fountain Bar**, set around the rather spectacular central fountain in Nam Phou Place, offers open-air dining on Lao and Chinese food, along with a very cooling spray when the evening breezes turn; and the **"Russian Bar,"** a large rustic barn-like place set on the riverfront near the intersection of Fa Ngum and Nokeo Khoumane streets, not only has excellent budget-priced Lao and Western food but also an open verandah with fantastic views of the Mekong River sunsets.

As for Lao and Chinese food, there are a great many places to choose from. Among the best: **Ban Phim** (ℂ (21) 3502) on Thanon Luang Prabang; the **Mekong Restaurant** (ℂ (21) 2339) on Thanon Thadeua; the **Snake Bar** (ℂ (21) 3617) on Thanon Nong Bone; and the **Nokkeo Latrymai Restaurant** (ℂ (21) 3159) toward the airport on Thanon Luang Prabang. Among other Asian speciality places, the **Dao Vieng** (ℂ (21) 3009) at 40 Thanon Heng Boun is one of the city's leading Chinese restaurants; the nearby **Nang Souri Noodle Shop** at 12–14 Thanon Heng Boun combines Chinese and Thai cuisine; the **Noorjahan** at 370 Thanon Samsentha and The Taj on Thanon Pang Kham, just north of the fountain square, are excellent Indian restaurants; and the Lan Xang Hotel's **Suki-yaki Restaurant**, right opposite the hotel on the riverfront, doesn't serve Japanese food at all, but Lao and Thai cuisine with exotic little delights like braised spiny ant-eater and "bleeding moose."

WHERE TO PLAY

As social codes have relaxed in Vientiane, most of the hotels have opened nightclubs, or dancing establishments — the clubs at the Anou, Lan Xang and Ekalath Metropole among the most popular. There's also a big private restaurant/disco called the **Viengla-ty Mai** on Lan Xang avenue toward the Pratuxai monument which is crowded most nights. You'll meet the modern young Laos at these places, and watch them switch effortlessly from the tango to the Thai *ram-*

wong to the boogie as the evening thunders on. If you're single, a quiet word to the waiters will produce a Lao girl to chat and dance with. But you'll have to appreciate that nightclubbing in Vientiane is still a rather innocent form of social life. In other words, don't count on anything more than that.

GETTING THERE

Thai International and Lao Aviation operate daily flights to Vientiane from Bangkok, and Vietnam Airlines flies regularly from Hanoi and Saigon. To get there from Bangkok by train and river ferry, check with the list of recommended travel agents on page 208.

GETTING AWAY

Lao Aviation operates all internal flights in Laos with a mixture of Russian and Chinese prop-driven aircraft and short-haul Russian troop helicopters. When I was there, you could really only book a flight to Pakse, the Plain of Jars or Luang Prabang through a Vientiane travel agent — they're the only people who can arrange the permits to go beyond Vientiane province. Lao Aviation (ℂ (21) 2093) has domestic and international booking offices on Thanon Pang Kham, just around from the Lan Xang Hotel.

INFORMATION

Inter-Lao Tourisme on Setthathirat street near the fountain square provides very good maps of Vientiane and the whole country, along with a cheaply produced but quite comprehensive little guidebook called *Welcome to Laos*. Also, the Women's International Group produces an annual *Vientiane Guide* which is mainly for incoming expatriate families but is also of great help to tourists. You can buy it in most hotels, and the proceeds go to support aid projects for women and children.

PAKSE

Pakse is a relatively prosperous administrative center and market town lying in a balmy, sub-tropical landscape of rice paddies and groves of palms at the confluence of the Mekong and See Don rivers in southern Laos. Built as recently as 1905, this capital of Champasak province has very little history of its own but is the gateway to the former royal capital of Champasak and perhaps the most important religious site in Southeast Asia — Wat Phu. It's also a key access to one of the widest and most picturesque sections of the Mekong River. When I was there, foreigners had to fly to Pakse on an individual or group tour from Vientiane — but, with the right permit, arranged before leav-

itself, Pakse lays claim to one of the most charming old French colonial landmarks anywhere in Indo-China, a former mansion which is now the Auberge du Champa.

WHAT TO SEE

Wat Phu
The ruins of this ancient temple lie 37 km (23 miles) from Pakse on the lower eastern slope of Phu Kao, a sacred mountain with a peak that's said to resemble a linga. The mountain is essential to Wat Phu's special

ing Vientiane, they could cross by ferry to Chongmek in Thailand and fly back to Bangkok from Ubon, 76 km (47 miles) east of there. It may well be possible to enter Laos that way now, integrating Pakse and Wat Phu into a general temple tour of northeast Thailand.

Despite its fairly lush riverine setting, Pakse has little to distinguish it from other Lao or Thai market towns, but as you enter it you get a sense of its strategic role on the edge of former pomp and splendor. On the outskirts of the city center, across one of two major bridges, a dilapidated but still quite majestic former royal villa stands over the river — slated, I was told, to be restored as an up-market tourist hotel. Within the town

status as a religious site — the monolith on top of it attracting Khmer Shivaites who built the first temple there well before the rise of the Khmer Empire. In the sixth century, a Chinese chronicle spoke of a temple on the site guarded by a thousand soldiers and dedicated to a spirit to whom the king offered a human sacrifice each year. Evidence suggests that it was also the principal temple of the capital of Chenla, Shreshthapura, which is believed to have been located on the site of present-day Champasak. As its name suggests, this in turn may previously have been part of the central Vietnam kingdom of Champa.

ABOVE: Temple carving at the Wat Phu Khmer ruins near Pakse.

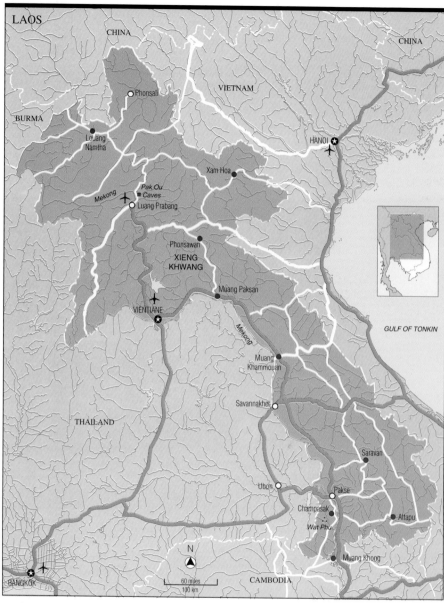

As possibly the oldest religious site used by the Khmer Hindus, Wat Phu is significant, indeed. And its antiquity is all the more pronounced by the state it's in today. Of its two imposing main palaces, built on a terrace at the foot of the hill, only the outer walls are still standing and their entrances, featuring elaborately sculptured gables, have all but collapsed — the huge stones tumbling as though struck by an earthquake. Beyond them, a series of steep stone stairways, also in a state of ruin, lead up the hillside to terraces where pavilions, a library and as many as six other buildings once stood. The main sanctuary, located on the highest terrace, is relatively well preserved, featuring an antechamber and side-naves with walls and lintels decorated with carved *devatas* and *dvarapalas*. Close by, against the foot of a cliff, there's a bas-relief carving of Shiva flanked by Brahma and Vishnu and, nearby, a huge flat stone with the outline of a crocodile carved deeply into it. Guides will describe how the outline neatly embraces the human body, and how a channel in the stone was put there to drain the blood — supporting the theory that this was in fact the altar upon which the early monarchs performed their human sacrifices.

The present ruins of Wat Phu are said to date back to the eleventh and twelfth centuries. Three Buddha images now stand in the sanctuary, and it is suggested that this may well be Southeast Asia's oldest Buddhist temple, too. The temple's key festival,

by boat beyond Champasak. It's known that the temple dates back to around 889 AD, and was dedicated to Durga, consort of Shiva in her terrible aspect. But time and the elements, not to mention looters, have wreaked a violent toll, all but destroying the temple complex except for the broken walls and traces of three towers of one of halls. Other relics — a lintel decorated with an image of Indra, and a stone linga with four faces at its head — are scattered among the trees.

Champasak, the docking point for the journey to Wat Phu, tells you little about its

staged in the three days leading up to the February full moon, coincides with the Buddhist Makha Puja. Another festival held each June climaxes with the sacrificial slaughter of a buffalo. But throughout the complex, much of the architecture and surviving decoration is definitely Hindu.

The best way to get to Wat Phu is by boat along the Mekong from Pakse, and this trip, favored by the tour agencies, usually combines the temple tour with visits to the region's two other principal attractions, Champasak itself and another temple ruin, **Huei Thamo**.

The site of this late ninth century ruin lies in dense secondary forest close to a small riverside village about two and a half hours

former glory as a royal capital, but exhibits some of the most striking examples of old French civic architecture — now showing considerable disrepair, of course — virtually cheek-to-jowl with modern stilted, tin-roofed wooden Lao homes. The town lies on either side of a red-dirt road that runs parallel with the river until it makes an abrupt right-turn and becomes part of the triumphal approach to Wat Phu. Along the way you'll see two gaudily decorated Buddha images built into the trunks and lower branches of trees. In the wide plain that lies before Wat Phu, another decrepit royal villa

ABOVE: Ruins of Wat Phu temple complex LEFT sprawl across a wide plain below Phu Cao. RIGHT: Pakse woman prepares sticky rice.

— a summer pavilion — lies on the edge of a large lotus pool, left to fall into ruin since the last king of Laos, Savang Vatthana, and his queen disappeared into the murky gulag of socialist re-education.

The standard tour of this region involves a boat trip to Huei Thamo, then the return trip to Champasak where a car or mini-van is usually waiting to take you to Wat Phu. The whole tour takes in a full day, and the return to Pakse is generally by road via a vehicular ferry that crosses the Mekong at Champasak. What with these grand relics

of the Khmer culture, the quiet charm of Champasak and the stunningly beautiful vistas of the Mekong River and forested hills along the way, it's a day you'll remember for a long time.

WHERE TO STAY

If the old royal villa in Pakse has indeed been restored, it's likely that this will be the most pleasurable hotel in town. At the time I visited, there was a new hotel under construction on the road from the villa to the town

center. Other than that, there really are only two hotels to choose from.

The **Souksamlane**, right in the center of town, is where the tour agencies put most foreign customers — it has comfortable air-conditioned rooms at US$18 a night with balconies overlooking the street and a friendly ground floor restaurant which provides mainly Lao food but some Western dishes.

But for my money, the **Auberge du Champa**, a couple of blocks from the Souksamlane on the way to the central market, is the place to stay. A converted colonial villa, it has comfort, charm, an air of antiquity and a powerful sense of what life must have been like in old Indo-China — the woven bamboo walls and ceiling of its ground-floor bar, the sculptured stonework of its patio, the vast wire-netted balcony restaurant upstairs, the geckos and the lazy ceiling fans, all of it carrying you back to another time. A new single-storey annex has been built around the main house and it still somehow manages to retain its charm. A spacious double room here will cost you US$30 to US$40 a night.

There's another large hotel, the **Pakse**, downtown near the market, but one look at it tells you to steer clear — it's a converted cinema, and quite an ugly establishment.

GETTING THERE AND AWAY

Lao Aviation operates a daily service to Pakse, and it may be possible to travel there by ferry from Vientiane — a trip which takes one day and one night, but requires a special permit, issued in Vientiane, and is probably restricted to Lao nationals. With the right permit, you can certainly depart by ferry and road to Ubon in Thailand. It may also be possible by now to travel by ferry from Pakse to the other key center of this southern region, Savannakhet.

XIENG KHWANG (PLAIN OF JARS)

Phonsawan, the new capital of northern Xieng Khwang province, reminds me of the rugged, undeveloped frontier towns that you find on the lower Tibet plateau in China.

ABOVE: Transport on the Mekong River near Pakse. OPPOSITE: The fabled Plain of Jars TOP. BOTTOM Market scene in Xieng Khwang.

The city was built after the former capital, Xieng Khwang was virtually destroyed by bombing during the campaign against the communist Pathet Lao in the Vietnam War. It's a sprawling, nondescript market town lying at the center of a vast, defoliated, dusty plain that still shows the scars of the bombing, and in the dry season the winds that sweep across the area are distinctly cold in the daytime and bitter at night.

But Phonsawan is the gateway to the country's unique historical attraction, the large stone jars that lie scattered across a grassy slope about 12 km (seven and a half miles) from town, close to a Lao air force base. Weighing as much as six tons, these mysterious vessels point to the sky like fat siege mortars, which more than one observer has cynically suggested the United States bomber pilots mistook them for. They're said to be many hundreds of years old, but beyond that no-one has really come up with a definite explanation for them.

One theory is that they were wine fermentation jars put there by a sixth century resistance hero to celebrate his victory over a despotic local ruler. Another is that they were burial jars. Yet another explanation may well lie in the region's arid character during the winter months — were they, in fact, nothing more than water storage vessels? Whatever, they tease the imagination, and they are one of those strange cultural attractions which draw visitors simply to be able to say they've seen it.

According to local reports, there were once several thousand jars at several sites across the region, but less than 100 now remain in two groups scattered on a hillock and across the floor of a shallow valley.

The Phonsawan authorities are obviously trying to develop a tourist industry centered on the jars and hilltribe and hot springs locations elsewhere in the region. The flight from Vientiane is certainly something not to be missed — the prop-driven Yak aircraft carrying you over the vivid physical contrasts of the rice-plains around Vientiane, then incredibly beautiful mountain ranges featuring many rivers and literally dozens of potential white-water rafting spots, and a vast reservoir, Ang Nam Ngum, and hydroelectric plant which not only serves domestic power needs but exports electricity to Thailand. Quite frankly though, Phonsawan itself has little to offer aside from the mysterious novelty of the Plain of Jars.

WHERE TO STAY AND WHERE TO EAT

Phonsawan's tourist facilities are not bad, considering the unsophisticated nature of the town. There's a modern 50-room hotel called the **Plain of Jars**, usually used by Diethelm tour groups, near the jars themselves, and at last report it was charging US$8 a night for double rooms. The government guesthouse on the western edge of town stands alone on a hilltop in a bleak landscape that reminded me of outback

Australia. It's closed a lot of the time and only opens when tourists turn up, and its rooms are basic. Not only that, but it has a communal cold-water bathroom and the electricity is available only from 6 to 9 pm at night. But apart from that, it's not such a bad place, and it's a good viewpoint for savagely beautiful sunsets created by the region's dust.

In "downtown" Phonsawan, the **Hayhin Hotel** is cozier and caters for visiting foreign aid officials. You can get a room there for about US$2 a night. Right across the road, the **Phonesaysouron Restaurant**, the town's only reasonable dining spot, serves a fixed but wholesome Lao supper and breakfasts of thick coffee and fried sesame buns.

LUANG PRABANG

To arrive in Luang Prabang, the most celebrated old royal capital of Laos, is to fly into one of Asia's most beautiful cities. As the plane from Vientiane circles before nosing down to the airport runway it's as though the city is one big tropical garden, the waters of the Mekong and Nam Khan rivers flashing amid the palms and other foliage, old French villas and civic buildings nestling here and there in the trees and the gold-leafed spires of its many temples sparkling in the sun. For many years, Luang Prabang ranked with mythical Shangri-la

Luang Prabang — "one big tropical garden".

as a fabled but virtually forbidden destination in Asia, difficult to get to even during the war, out of reach completely during the revolutionary years and only now wide open to foreigners.

From the ground it's even more idyllic. The road into town from the airstrip passes rows of neat timber shophouses, temple walls and weathered colonial buildings, all set among trees, with the city's highest pagoda, Wat Chom Si, atop a steep hill in the center of town, providing a dramatic backdrop all the way. To describe it as a

laid-back place would be an understatement: even the people look as though they're enjoying a permanent siesta, the only real activity occurring in the early morning and late afternoon when shop assistants and government employees cycle to and from work.

The Mekong and Nam Khan rivers converge at the western end of Luang Prabang, shaping the town like the head and beak of a large bird. The downtown "business" district, where you'll find Lao Aviation, Inter-Lao Tourisme, the GPO, National Museum and market, lies along the crest and beak

ABOVE: Meo hilltribe women in Luang Prabang. OPPOSITE: The beautiful National Museum, formerly the Royal Palace.

between the temple hill, Phu Si, and the Mekong. This long riverfront area is also where the main temples are located.

Luang Prabang has so many fine and historic temples that you can get tired of going from one to the next. To forestall that, I've provided the history and main features of the five best ones. The oldest temple site, Wat Visoun, dates back to 1513, shortly before the first Lao kingdom of Lan Xang was established here by the warlord Fa Ngum. The city's glory lasted only 12 years, until 1545 when the capital moved to Vientiane, but it remained a seat and power base of Lao royalty right up until 1975 when the Pathet Lao hauled the last monarch, Savang Vattana, off to probable execution somewhere in the north.

You can walk or bicycle all over Luang Prabang, quickly becoming familiar with its simple grid of streets and main attractions. The people are friendly but also quite reserved: you can tell from the way they nonchalantly accept foreigners in their midst, without getting excited, that they've been acquainted with tourism for many years. As this is the Angkor Wat of Laos, it's very much part of a daily tourist conveyer belt that runs from Vientiane, with Lao Aviation operating daily flights full of tour groups and even pulling aircraft off other routes to provide extra services if the traffic gets too big. Again, you probably still have to arrange an individual or group tour from Vientiane, with the necessary permits, to go there.

WHAT TO SEE

National Museum

This, the former royal palace, is an opulent French-Lao mansion with a decorated central tower, extending from Phu Si to the Mekong riverfront. Originally constructed in 1904 as the official residence of King Sisavang Vong, father of the ill-fated last monarch, it is literally packed with relics and treasures of the dynastic era and Lao Buddhism. It main hall, with its ornately decorated walls and high ceiling stuns you the moment you walk in, as do its key exhibits, the dais of the former Supreme Patriarch of Laos and a series of obviously priceless Buddha images, including

a reclining Buddha and a standing image made of marble. The sense of awe heightens as you step into the throne room beyond, where the throne itself, the king's elephant saddle and other royal vestments, along with a collection of gold and crystal Buddhas, are on show in a vast hall so elaborately decorated that you can get quite dizzy studying the walls.

Other images and treasures fill the large reception halls to the right and left of the entrance. On the right, the king's reception hall features busts of the various Lao mon-

archs, screens depicting the *Ramayana* and walls decorated with dramatic murals of traditional Lao life painted 70 years ago by the French artist Alix de Fautereau. Beyond that, in another exhibition room, a large gold Buddha called the Pha Bang, presented to Fa Ngum by his Khmer benefactors when he conquered Luang Prabang, stands amid ivory Buddhas fashioned from elephant tusks, a host of other sculptures, a temple frieze and three embroidered silk screens featuring Buddhist stories.

PREVIOUS PAGE: Gilded artistry of Wat Sen, typical of the Buddhist heritage of Luang Prabang. ABOVE: Traditional weavings have become a tourist attraction at Ban Khanom, outside Luang Prabang. OPPOSITE: Prayer hall of Wat Xieng Thong.

To the left of the entrance, next to the queen's reception hall, there's a room crowded with exhibits of various official gifts given by foreign heads of state and VIPs over the years. What's fascinating about it is the sort of kitsch that royalty and government leaders give each other — stuff that most people would probably keep in the attic or unload at a jumble sale. Suffice to say that a cheap scale model of the Apollo moon vehicle Columbia, presented by Richard Nixon, is probably the classiest exhibit on show.

Viewing all this wealth and finery, it's not difficult to sympathize with the communist guerrillas who crushed the monarchy the moment they triumphed, remembering of course that Savang Vatthana gave his royal blessing to the United States bombing and covert counter-insurgency program in Laos during the war. But when you stroll through the royal apartments to the rear of the throne and reception rooms, the human element and the sense of pathos in old sepia photographs of the royal family in happier times, especially a misty Dietrich-style print of the queen, counter-balances the moral and political issue. The bedrooms, too, once the home and sanctuary of children, and the king's bathroom — so functional, austere and coldly tiled that it must have been murder on winter mornings — somehow they inspired me to images of the Romanovs huddled together in the cellar as the Bolshevik executioners strode in. No one outside the highest echelons of the government really knows what became of King Vatthana and his queen, but it's quietly accepted that they were put to death in 1977 for refusing to support the revolutionary regime's policies.

The Temple Tour
In one respect, **Wat Chom Si** is the most spectacular temple in Luang Prabang — commanding the town from its perch high on the peak of Phu Si. But the viewpoint is the main attraction, the panorama you enjoy of the entire city from the lower terrace of its stupa. It's wonderful up there at sunset, watching the colors change right across the city and its river stretches. On a ridge close to the temple there's an old

revolving Russian anti-aircraft gun left over from the early revolutionary days. Down below, **Wat Xieng Thong** (Golden City Temple), located right on the confluence of the two rivers, is considered the city's finest — a large complex of shrines, pavilions and prayer halls which feature, among other things, brilliant and quite unusual mosaics and rare gilded erotic carvings taken from the Ramayana. Among the other treasures at this 400-year-old site are a pavilion packed with Buddha images and a huge gilded royal funeral chariot

National Museum is said to have been found in this stupa.

Wat Mai, close to the GPO off Luang Prabang's east-west main street, Thanon Phothiserat, is a relatively new temple, built in 1796. Its five-tiered roof and gilded sculptured door panels depicting scenes from the life of Buddha and the *Ramayana* are among its key architectural features. The compound also houses two shallow-draft traditional barges which lead celebrations on the rivers during the Lao New Year in April and Water Festival in October.

with dragon heads rearing from its prow, another containing a reclining Buddha dating back to the temple's construction in 1560 and, at one corner of the complex, a royal barge.

Wat Visoun, south of Phu Si near the Rama Hotel, is even older than Xieng Thong, originally built in 1513. Its main features are a collection of fifteenth century ordination stones, a display of wooden Buddhas sculpted in a style called "Calling for Rain" and the dramatic white That Pathum (Lotus Stupa) in front of the main hall, known more popularly as That Mak Mo (Watermelon Stupa) because of its bulbous shape. The collection of small gold and crystal Buddhas in the throne room of the

Wat That Luang, built in 1818 on a hill to the east of the city, has a central stupa containing the ashes of King Sisavang Vong.

Across the Mekong River from central Luang Prabang you'll find a complex of smaller temples that include **Wat Tham**, built into a limestone cave, and **Wat Chom Phet**, which provides another dramatic panorama of the town and river.

Pak Ou Caves

These Buddhist grottoes lie 30 km (19 miles) west along the Mekong River, and the trip there provides another insight into the beauty and menace of this great waterway, especially in the dry season when your boatman has to continually dodge currents and whirlpools created by the low water. On the way, the squat, shallow-draft tour boats call into a small village which is famous for its traditional rice wine stills. You can watch the fiery concoction being distilled and also enjoy a tipple or two, fortifying yourself with the powerful essence for the rest of the trip ahead.

At Pak Ou, there are two large caves in a sheer limestone cliff right over the river, both containing terraces filled with **Buddha images** of all shapes, styles and sizes. There

its **cotton and silk weaving**, and you can watch the women working on traditional looms and also haggle with the vendors in a small central market pavilion. The quality of the weaving is very good, the prices very reasonable — and the center is part of a local government campaign to restore traditional arts and crafts.

WHERE TO STAY

A new hotel, the **Villa de la Princesse** (**(** 7041) set in a stylishly renovated former

used to be a lot more: Pak Ou was one of the prime targets of thievery and smuggling rackets which saw many of the treasures of Laos spirited out to the United States and the West during the war. Beyond Pak Ou there's another spectacular limestone cliff where the Nam Ou River joins the Mekong, and the tour boats generally make a short trip along there before returning to Luang Prabang.

Ban Phanom

This small village east of the city is Luang Prabang's souvenir stop, where all tours, individual or group, inevitably end up. But it's well worth going there. Ban Thanom, populated by the Lu minority, is famous for

royal mansion on Rue Sakkarine, is the pride of Luang Prabang's tourist industry. It has rooms that are deluxe by Lao standards, furnishings and decorations that are said to have come from the royal collection, a quiet grassed courtyard for cocktails and buffets, an upstairs verandah bar with a view of the surrounding streetlife and regular performances of traditional Lao court and tribal dancing. The tariff when I was there was US$40 a night.

Elsewhere, the sprawling **Phousy Hotel**, located at the town's main intersection

OPPOSITE: Buddha images pack the sacred Pak Ou Caves downriver from Luang Prabang. ABOVE (LEFT): Five-star comfort of the Villa de la Princesse Hotel. RIGHT: Poolside at the Luang Prabang Hotel.

where Phothisarat and Setthathirat streets meet, is an older tourist hotel with rooms in the US$25 to US$30 range and surrounding gardens with an open-air bar. The **Mitta Phab**, set on a hill to the east of the town, has a swimming pool and deluxe rooms at between US$25 and US$60 a night. It also has superb views of Luang Prabang. The **Rama Hotel** near the central market has the advantage of being right in town and featuring one of Luang Prabang's very few nightclub/dancing halls, while another new hotel, the **Muang Sua**, has recently

weighed in with rooms at US$25 to US$30 a night.

WHERE TO EAT

As in most Indo-Chinese cities, the main hotels offer the best and most reliable restaurants in Luang Prabang, serving Lao, Chinese and Western food. Otherwise, the **Young Koun Restaurant**, opposite the Rama Hotel and Wat Visoun, is crowded with Laos and foreigners every night and its popularity is matched by the variety and standard of its menu.

ABOVE and RIGHT: Rustic Luang Prabang — village hut and sunset on the Mekong.

Travelers'
Tips

GETTING THERE

Travel to Indo-China is getting progressively easier and more efficient as the region opens up to the rest of the world. But as yet, it's not really regarded as a destination in its own right, and most visitors include it as the adventure section of a general Asian jaunt. In this respect, Hong Kong has become the main Asian access point for Vietnam and Bangkok the gateway to Laos and Cambodia.

At the time of writing, there were only two direct long-haul air services to the region — Air France from Paris and Aeroflot from Moscow. But with the United States embargo likely to be lifted, three of America's leading carriers, Northwest, United and Delta, were known to be preparing for direct services to Vietnam. Otherwise, Western airlines like Lufthansa, SAS and Finnair were offering services to Hanoi, Saigon (Ho Chi Minh City), Vientiane and Phnom Penh with connections on Asian carriers from Hong Kong and Bangkok. Regionally based carriers like Cathay Pacific, Singapore Airlines, Garuda Indonesia and Philippine Airlines were also providing long-haul services from the United States and Britain, linking up with regional flights into Vietnam from Hong Kong, Bangkok, Singapore, Jakarta and Manila.

Regional services into Vietnam are growing as fast as the Asian carriers can conclude joint-service agreements with Vietnam Airlines, and Cathay Pacific, Philippine Airlines, Thai International, Garuda Indonesia, Royal Brunei, Singapore Airlines and Malaysian Airlines are among those providing direct flights to Hanoi and Saigon. Thai International's daily services from Bangkok to Saigon and Hanoi, and Cathay Pacific's daily flights from Hong Kong to Ho Chi Minh City (with four flights a week to Hanoi) are regarded as virtual goldmines by both carriers, packed with business travelers. Both services are run in cooperation with Vietnam Airlines. Thai International also operates daily flights from Bangkok to Vientiane and three flights a day to Phnom Penh, again in cooperation with Lao Aviation and Kampuchea Airlines. Hong Kong's Dragonair was also due to start a direct service to Phnom Penh in 1993.

Within Indo-China, the three national airlines operate daily services linking Hanoi, Saigon, Vientiane and Phnom Penh, along with long-haul services to Moscow.

IMMIGRATION AND CUSTOMS

Things have changed since the days when only overseas consulates provided visas to Vietnam, Laos and Cambodia. Vietnam now gives out two-month tourist visas and actually grants visas on arrival in Hanoi or

Saigon, but it's usually a crowded, frustrating bureaucratic process and costs US$75 to complete. In terms of time and convenience, you'd be much better off arranging visas before you travel, and this means contacting a mainstream tour company or one of a growing crop of smaller specialist Indo-China tour agencies which have sprung up across the world since the doors to the region opened. The alternative is to arrange visas in Hong Kong or Bangkok, but wait around for five to seven days for your tour operator to get it approved.

The reason you have to go to a tour operator is that all three countries prefer visitors to come in on a group tour. It means better control, and it ensures that their national tourist organizations earn foreign-exchange from domestic ground-handling services. But it's not as strict and monopolistic as it seems. Vietnam not only grants visas on arrival, it's now dealing with so

OPPOSITE: Fish market on the Cai River in Vietnam's historic Hoi An. ABOVE: Schoolgirls in traditional *ao dais* in central Saigon.

many multiple-entry business travelers that it allows single-entry tourists to come in as they please. But then, it maintains a system of travel permits within the country that makes sure you're kept under the official thumb. In short, while you can get into Vietnam on your own, you still need the services of government-operated agencies like Saigon Tourism, Hanoi Tourism and Vietnam Tourism to arrange the necessary travel and police permits for in-country tours. Most of the better hotels in Vietnam have in-house travel branches which will

Also, you no longer have to travel to Vientiane by air. Visitors are now free to take the overnight train from Bangkok to Nong Khai and enter via the Mekong River ferry crossing. One warning, though: all tourist visas are restricted to 15 days, and at the time of writing there were no extensions. If you wanted to travel longer in Laos, you had to go back to Bangkok and start again, or pay the fine of US$5 per day for overstaying.

Cambodia grants two-month visas, and again it's no use going to a consulate. The procedure is the same as for Laos — arrange

arrange everything with the government bodies. In early 1993, however, a Saigon newspaper reported that the government was considering abolishing internal travel permits altogether.

Getting into Laos is quite easy, but it requires a little subterfuge to keep costs down. Lao consulates will not issue a visa, and you have to go to a tour agency to get one. This can be quite expensive: Diethelm in Bangkok, for example, charge around US$1,100 for just a two-day visit to Vientiane. So, what you do is arrange a two-day visit with a cheaper tour company and, once in Vientiane, go to a local agency and book a tour that takes in Luang Prabang, the Plain of Jars, Pakse or wherever else you want to go.

flights, visa and even internal travel (Siem Reap and Angkor Wat) with an outside tour agency, or book just the visa and international flight and let a local company do the rest once you're in Phnom Penh. In early 1993 the government had started issuing eight-day visas costing US$20 on arrival in Phnom Penh, and the word was that they could be extended to up to one month at no extra cost.

Customs requirements for all three countries look intimidating at first glance — a typical struggle with socialist regulations and paperwork. But that's all it is — forms in triplicate. The only real problem to worry about is Vietnam's paranoia about photographers and film-makers, a problem that stems from a couple of politically dodgy Hong Kong Chinese film productions that have angered the government. Hence, if you're filming with a video 8 or Hi8 camera, even if it's just standard holiday stuff, check with your tour operator before departure — you may have to go along to the Ministry of Culture first and have the videocassettes viewed and bonded to get them through customs.

TOUR COMPANIES

As the key gateways to Indo-China, both Bangkok and Hong Kong have an increasing number of tour companies offering packages with visas included. On the basis of cost, customer-relations and efficiency, I would recommend the following:

HONG KONG TO VIETNAM

Tulips Travel, 303 Supreme House, 2A Hart Avenue, Tsimshatsui, Kowloon. ((852) 2367-8303. Fax: (852) 2367-6210. This very reputable company also has a New York office and United States toll-free number. **Friendship E. Travel**, 6th floor, room 604, Mohan's Building, 14–16 Hankow Road, Tsimshatsui, Kowloon. ((852) 2312-1888. Fax: (852) 366-1623.

HONG KONG TO VIETNAM/LAOS/CAMBODIA

Wallem Travel Ltd, 46th floor, Hopewell Center, 183 Queen's Road East, Hong Kong. ((852) 2865-1618. Fax: (852) 2865-2652.

BANGKOK TO VIETNAM/LAOS/CAMBODIA

Diethelm Travel, Kian Gwan Building II, 140 Wireless Road, Bangkok 10500. ((662) 255-9150. Fax: (66-2) 256-0248.
Indoswiss, 1102B 11th floor, Dusit Thani Building, 946 Rama IV Road, Bangkok. ((662) 236-7655.
Thai Indo-China Supply Co., 4th floor, 79 Pan Road, Silom, Bangkok. ((66-2) 234-1555.
Viet Tour Holidays, 1717 Lard-Prao Road, Samsennok, Huay-Kwang, Bangkok 10310. ((66-2) 511-3272. Fax: (66-2) 511-3357.

BANGKOK TO LAOS/CAMBODIA

M.K. Ways (Thailand) Co Ltd, 57/11 Witthayu Road, Bangkok 10330. ((66-2) 254-4765. Fax: (66-2) 254-5583. This company has a tiny branch right opposite the main gate to the Lao embassy in Bangkok, and I can thoroughly recommend it for efficient budget travel into Laos and Cambodia. For Laos, M.K. Ways will arrange the visa (it takes five working days) and return first-class rail travel to Nong Khai, then leave it

to you to make your own tour arrangements in Vientiane. For Cambodia, it'll arrange travel to Phnom Penh and the visa (three days) or a full five-day tour package in Phnom Penh and Angkor Wat.

INTERNATIONAL TOUR AGENCIES

UNITED STATES

Tulips Travel, 420 Lexington Avenue, Suite 2738, New York, NY 10171-0094. ((212)

OPPOSITE: Buddhist monks at Thien Mu Pagoda in Hue. ABOVE: Village girl distills rice wine in village outside Luang Prabang.

490-3388. Fax: (212) 490-3580. Toll-free: (800) 882-3388.
Mekong Travel, 151 First Avenue, Suite 172, New York, NY 10003, ((212) 420-1586.
Budgetours International, 8907 Westminster Avenue, Garden Grove, CA 92644. ((213) 465-7315.

AUSTRALIA

Orbitours, 7th floor, Dymock's Building, 428 George Street, Sydney 2000. ((61-2) 221-7322. Fax: (61-2) 221-7459

NEW ZEALAND

Destinations, 2nd floor, Premier Building, 4 Durham Street, Auckland. ((64-9) 390464.

BRITAIN

Regent Holidays (UK) Ltd, 13 Small Street, Bristol BS1 1DE. ((44-272) 211711. Fax: (0272) 254866.

FRANCE

HitVoyages, 21 rue des Bernardins, 75005 Paris. ((33-1) 43 54 17 17.

SWITZERLAND

Exotissimo, 8 Avenue du Mal, 1205 Geneva. ((41-22) 812166. Fax: (41-22) 812171.

GERMANY

Indoculture Tours,Bismarkplatz 1 D-7000 Stuttgart 1. ((49-711) 617057.

AUSTRIA

View Travel, Sankt Voitgasse 9, A-1130 Vienna. ((43-22) 831-8532.

TOUR AGENCIES IN VIETNAM

Within Vietnam, the main city offices of the Vietnam National Administration of Tourism, which has a monopoly on domestic travel arrangements for foreigners, are:

Hanoi Tourism, 18 Ly Thuong Kiet, Hanoi. ((84-4) 54209.
Saigon Tourist, 17 Lam Son Square, Ho Chi Minh City. ((84-8) 224-987.

There are some independent tour agencies now operating in Saigon, though they all act as agents for Saigon Tourist. The most helpful and reputable are as follows:
Eden Tourist, Eden Trading Center, 104-106 Nguyen Hue Avenue, Saigon. ((84-8) 292589. Fax: (84-8) 230783.
Far East Tourist, 61 Le Thanh Ton Street, Saigon. ((84-8) 225187. Fax: (84-8) 295361.
Travel Agency, 110 Nguyen Hue Avenue, Saigon. ((84-8) 293 678. Fax: (84-8) 225538

In Hanoi, there's one independent company which has already built a reputation for excellent multilingual service:
BS Company Ltd, 72 Ba Trieu Street, Hanoi. ((84-4) 262386. Fax: (84-4) 269285.

TOUR AGENCIES IN LAOS

In Laos, several small privately operated tour companies have opened in Vientiane to handle foreign tourists, but they all simply act as marketing and booking agents for the state tourism monopoly, Inter-Lao Tourism. However, you'll find they're friendly, accommodating and quite efficient, with subsidiary agents in all main cities and cultural centers ready to take care of you the moment you step down from the plane. I would recommend the following:
Raja Tour, Second floor, Anou Hotel, 01-03 Heng Boon Street, Vientiane, P.O. Box 3655. ((856-21) 3660. Fax: (856-21) 9378.
Diethelm Travel, Setthathirat Road, Nam Phu Square, Vientiane, P.O. Box 2657. ((856-21) 4442/5911. Telex: 4491 TEVTELS Diethelm Laos.
Lao Air Booking Co Ltd, 38-40 Setthathirat Road, Vientiane, P.O. Box 3080. ((856-21) 5331. Fax: (856-21) 5331.
Aerocontact Asia Co Ltd, 14 Fa Ngum Road, Vientiane. P.O. Box 4300. ((856-21) 3613. Fax: (856-21) 2604.

OPPOSITE: To travel between Saigon and Hanoi, you can take the Reunification Train or brave the arduous public bus system.

TOUR AGENCIES IN CAMBODIA

Cambodia's domestic tour companies act as ground-handling agents for international operators and also arrange independent itineraries — mainly to Angkor Wat. As of early 1995, it was considered risky to try traveling to any other centers outside Phnom Penh. Recommendations:

Multihappy Express Tour Co Ltd., 113 Street N°126, Phnom Penh. (Just down from Hotel

Indo-China. They can often be quite flexible, too. Lao Aviation and Kampuchea Airlines will add extra flights to their key cultural destinations, Luang Prabang and Angkor Wat, if the volume of tourists gets too big for scheduled services.

Their aircraft, however, are mainly old Soviet Tupolov 134 jets and Antonov and Yak propellor-driven planes; and it can be quite off-putting at first to sit aboard the cramped, noisy and often grubby Tupolovs, for example, and ponder signs on the bulkhead that say "Emergency Rope." Laos and

Ripole near the Central Market). ((855-23) 24688. Fax: (855-23) 26439.
Asian Thai Travel, 76 Street N°126, Phnom Penh. (Opposite Multihappy Express Tour Co). ((855-23) 23339.
Diethelm Travel (Cambodia) Ltd, 8 Lenin Boulevard, Phnom Penh. ((855-23) 26648. Fax: (855-23) 26676.

GETTING AROUND

BY AIR

The national carriers — Vietnam Airlines, Lao Aviation and Kampuchea Airlines — operate very efficient domestic networks in

Cambodia also fly old converted Soviet troop helicopters on shorter routes.

For all that, you get a good aerial bus ride to where you want to go, and despite reports to the contrary the safety record in all three countries is high when you consider the volume of passenger/flights. Modernization of all three networks is just around the corner: Vietnam, for instance, has been awaiting the lifting of the United States embargo to upgrade its fleet with new Boeings. Domestic airports right across the region are run-down and rustic, to say the least, but they serve food and drinks and they're not overly uncomfortable.

Airline booking offices in main cities are as follows:

Vietnam Airlines (International): 25 Trang Thi, Hanoi. ((84-4) 53842. 116 Nguyen Hue, Ho Chi Min (Saigon). ((84-8) 92118. **Vietnam Airlines** (Domestic): 16 Le Thai To, Hanoi, ((84-4) 55283. 27B Nguyen Dinh Chieu, Ho Chi Min (Saigon). ((84-8) 99910. **Lao Aviation**: 2 Pangkham Road, Vientiane, ((856-21) 2093, Fax: (856-21) 2093. **Kampuchea Airlines**: (Departement de l'Aviation Civil du Cambodge), 62 Tou Samouth Boulevard, Phnom Penh. ((855-23) 25887.

you can roll along in the open air aboard a pedal-cyclo, which you'll find just about everywhere you go in Indo-China, and will cost you about US$1 per hour ($10 a day). Otherwise, it's easy to hire motorcyles in Vientiane and Phnom Penh at about US$10 per day (24 hours), and most cities rent bicycles if you want to get around a little more sedately.

ACCOMMODATION

Hotels are improving rapidly as tourism

By Road

Hire cars, minibuses and limousines are available throughout the region, with the main hotels and tour companies operating them. If you're travelling independently, charges seem to be the same whether you're in Hanoi or Phnom Penh — around US$30 to US$50 a day, depending on whether it's a minibus or new Toyota. This includes gas and the driver's accommodation if there's an overnight stay.

Private taxis are available in most cities, on call around the main hotels, but these generally involve a lot of haggling over the fare. And why cram yourself into a taxicab when

grows in Indo-China, but you'll find there's still a big gap in comfort and service between the new international-class properties and those that survived the war. At the top of the range, you'll find the **Pullman Metropole** in Hanoi, **Saigon Floating Hotel** and **Century Hotel** in Saigon, **Parasol du Blanc** and **Asian Pavilion** in Vientiane and the **Cambodiana** and **Phnom Penh Floating Hotel** in Phnom Penh as good as any in Asia. Saigon's **Hotel Continental**, **Rex**, **Majestic** and **Doc Lap (Caravelle)** would be equally as good if they weren't state-owned, with the tendency to be inflex-

OPPOSITE: Century Hotel and typical river life in Hue. ABOVE: Lan Xang Hotel pool in Vientiane.

ible and often surly with their guests. Rates are high — ranging from US$120 to US$180 a night.

Below them, there's a wide level of old hotels and guesthouses which have either been renovated or still aspire to grander times — the fading **Lan Xang** and **Ekalath Metropole** in Vientiane, the **Bong Sen** in Saigon, the **Bac Nam** and **Dan Chu** hotels in Hanoi, and the **Hotel Royal** (formerly the famed Samaki) and **Hotel Sukhalay** in Phnom Penh. These establishments are air-conditioned, reasonably comfortable and

offer quite good restaurants and bars. They're the sort of places where bathroom water heaters sometimes go on the blink, taps suddenly don't work and wardrobe doors don't close properly; but for travelers with a sense of adventure, they're still far more reminiscent of old Indo-China than the new business hotels. Most of these mid-range hotels also offer the best value in rates — generally about US$35 to US$45 a night. Addresses and more details of the hotels mentioned above are in the WHERE TO STAY sections of the relevant destinations.

SECURITY

Indo-China requires the sort of precautions you'd take against theft anywhere else in the world — put anything of particular value in the hotel safe deposit, don't carry a lot of money on you in the streets, and keep that camera close to you at all times. Laos has a very low crime rate and, ironically, so

have Phnom Penh and Angkor Wat, but there are hotspots in Vietnam where you have to be especially careful. Saigon requires extra care at night, when gangs of homeless, dispossessed youths prowl the riverfront and darker streets. Their modus operandi is to crowd around a visitor and distract his or her attention while nimble fingers pick their way into handbags, belly-bags or back pockets. Theft from hotel rooms is not unknown, particularly in Saigon's older, more down-market hotels, and there have been several quite serious hotel thefts in Danang.

HEALTH

The standard of hygiene throughout Indo-China ranges from poor to appalling, and its health services are in a dilapidated state. Hepatitis is the most prevalent disease to guard against, and no-one should travel the region without prior vaccination. Although you'll find mosquito nets in most older hotels, malaria and encephalitis are common enough that you'll need encephalitis shots before travelling and a course of malaria pills while you're on the road. Cholera is also a problem, especially in Vietnam, so make sure you've got those shots up to date.

To put all this into perspective, these are the sort of health precautions that one would expect to take in any developing region. With prudence, the worst thing you'll have to safeguard yourself from is diarrhea, and the best way to do that is to drink only bottled water wherever you go and avoid drinks with ice in them outside your hotel. Most leading hotels have an in-house clinic or doctor on call for emergencies; otherwise you can take out travel insurance with the Hong Kong-and Singapore-based Asia Emergency Assistance, which has a joint venture in Vietnam providing, among other things, medical evacuation in event of serious illness or injury. You can contact AEA as follows:

Asia Emergency Assistance, 9th floor, Allied Capital Resources Building, 32–38 Ice House Street, Central, Hong Kong. ((852) 810 8898. Fax: (852) 845-0395.

EMERGENCY CLINICS

In **Hanoi**, the Vietnam-Sweden Health Cooperation Program operates a top-class clinic for locals and foreigners opposite the Swedish Embassy on So 2, Duang 358, Khu Van Phuc, Quan Ba Dinh. You can call ((4) 54824 or 54825 for details.

In **Saigon**, the Cho Ray Hospital at 210B Nguyen Chi Thanh Boulevarde has a clinic for foreigners with English-speaking doctors. ((8) 255137.

Vientiane has two emergency clinics available for foreigners attached to the Swedish and Australian embassies. Telephone numbers are: Swedish, ((21) 3421 (clinic), ((21) 3525 (after hours), ((21) 2922 (embassy); Australian, ((21) 4691 (clinic), ((21) 2183 (after hours), ((21) 2477 (embassy).

In **Phnom Penh**, the World Access Medical Services Clinic at 53B Street N°63, west off the city's main thoroughfare, Boulevarde Achar Mean, is one of a number of clinics for foreigners which have opened in the wake of the United Nations deployment. You can telephone it on ((23) 27045.

CURRENCY

In a region in which the currencies are called the *dong*, *kip* and *riel*, it's somewhat nice to know that the United States greenback will get you just about anything you want. The reason is that all three currences are worthless anywhere else. In 1992, the Vietnamese *dong* was running at around 12,000 to the United States dollar, the Lao kip at about 700 and in Phnom Penh a dollar would get you 2,000 or more riels. Laos and Cambodia were also accepting Thai baht as an alternative to the greenback.

In Vietnam, the government had introduced a new 10,000 *dong* note, making it considerably easier to carry local currency on you without feeling as though you'd robbed a bank. Or that someone might rob you. In Vientiane and Phnom Penh, you could pay for a meal in a restaurant with United States dollars and request your change in a mixture of dollars, Thai baht and the local currency — and get it all at the exact exchange rates.

As for currency exchange, most local and foreign joint-venture banks in Vietnam, along with the better-class hotels, will convert the main international currencies; but because of the United States embargo they wouldn't take American Express cards or travellers cheques when I was there. Virtually all hotels and restaurants in Laos and Cambodia wouldn't accept any cards at all, preferring cash on the nail. In Phnom Penh, black market currency exchange stalls

around the Central Market — apparently tolerated by the government — were offering between three and five points over the official exchange rate for the United States dollar.

COMMUNICATIONS

IDD telephone and fax services are now pretty common in the upper-market hotels in **Vietnam** and **Cambodia**, though an incoming or outgoing fax will often take up to 24 hours to get through in Vietnam. This is generally the time it takes for scrutineers in the Post Office to translate it before passing it on. However, there's no such petty censorship in Phnom Penh.

If your hotel in Vietnam doesn't have IDD or fax, properties like the Saigon Floating Hotel and Pullman Metropole will often let you use their Business Center

OPPOSITE: Ploughing with water buffalo in ricelands near Nha Trang. ABOVE: Farming near Da Nang.

facilities for a fee. Beyond that, there are at least two independent business centers, one in Hanoi and the other in Saigon, where you can get things done on a fee basis. They are:

Hanoi Business Center, 51 Ly Thai To, Hanoi. ((84-4) 266122. Fax: (84-4) 266030.

Saigon Business Center, 49 Dong Du, Ho Chi Min (Saigon). (Dong Du runs east off Dong Khoi, formerly Tu Do Street, opposite the Bong Sen Hotel). ((84-8) 298777. Fax: (84-4) 298155.

Office on the corner of Thanon Khou Viang and Lan Xang Avenue and book a line. This sometimes meant waiting for several hours, but you could arrange a fairly speedy call to Bangkok on a radiotelephone service.

ELECTRICITY

In most older hotels in Indo-China, it's amazing that the power circuits actually work. The wiring and sockets date back to the French era, and breakdowns are com-

Phnom Penh, likewise, has international telephone and fax services, with most hotels hooked up; but the system was not sophisticated enough to cope with the business and diplomatic traffic when I was there, and callers had to restrict their calls to three minutes.

In **Laos**, some of the better hotels have IDD and international fax services, but with only three lines out of the country — one through Hong Kong, another poor-quality system via Moscow and a satellite link via Australia you still had to use the operator when I was there. Full IDD service was due to begin in 1994, but otherwise the only way of getting a call or fax out was to go to the ITT exchange building at the General Post

mon. Moreover, Vietnam has two currents, 110 volts and 220 volts, depending what city you're in, with two-pin round-prong outlets for 100v and two-pin United States-type outlets for 220v. If you're taking a hairdryer, electric shaver or Handycam battery charger with you, make sure it's multisystem, 110-220v.

Laos and Cambodia are a lot simpler — it's 200 volts wherever you go, though the antiquated wiring may have you wondering about overloads and short-circuits. In Phnom Penh, particularly, black-outs occur quite regularly, and most older hotels provide candles in the rooms. Of course, it also means no air-conditioning when the power fails.

TIME

All three countries are GMT + 7.

PHOTOGRAPHY

You'll find plenty of shops and hotel boutiques in every city and main town of the region selling Kodak and Fuji film, along with specialist camera stores with all the up-to-date cameras and equipment. However, Kodakchrome and Fuji slide film isn't always easy to come by, and when buying film of any sort check the expiration date — you can easily get palmed off with film that should have been trashed a couple of years ago.

Most key airports now proudly label their X-ray machines "Film Safe," but if I were you I wouldn't trust them. Hand your film over in a polythene bag for security inspection.

CLOTHING

Light cotton tropical clothing is obviously most suitable for travel throughout Indo-China, though a pullover or light jacket should be carried if you're going to destinations such as Dalat in Vietnam's Central Highlands or the mountains of Laos — it can get quite chilly there at night. It's advisable to dress quite modestly — no revealing tank-tops or crotch-hugging shorts or hotpants. The Indo-Chinese get a kick out of fashionable foreigners, but do not appreciate semi-nudity.

TRADITIONS AND TABOOS

The Indo-Chinese are a very hospitable people, and quite flexible in their dealings with foreigners. This means that when problems or frustrations occur — and they will, just as the first travelers into mainland China found — you should try to treat the issue as problem-solving, not the flashpoint for anger. There's an innate and quite compatible sense of humor in this region which you won't find in east and northeast Asia, and in most cases it smooths out misunderstandings before they reach boiling point. As in China, it also helps to appreciate that these people are trying to recover the expertise and sophistication that they lost years ago, and a bit of patience and tolerance goes a long way. So does a smile.

The only real cultural imperative to take account of is Buddhist temple touring in each country. It's a mark of respect to dress for the occasion — shirts and slacks (or jeans) rather than shorts and tank-tops, and

women should cover their arms and legs. Monks and novices are also forbidden to accept anything directly, hand-to-hand, from women. In Laos and Cambodia, it's disrespectful to sit with your feet pointing at other people; and it's also not the done thing to touch or pat people on the head.

OPPOSITE: The tranquility of Indo-China — the Mekong in Luang Prabang. ABOVE: Monk and woolly hat in Luang Prabang's early morning chill.

Quick Reference A–Z Guide
to Places and Topics of Interest with Listed Accommodation, Restaurants and Useful Telephone Numbers